200 make ahead dishes

200 make ahead dishes

hamlyn **all color**

Sara Lewis

An Hachette UK Company
www.hachette.co.uk

First published in Great Britain in 2008 by Hamlyn,
a division of Octopus Publishing Group Ltd,
2–4 Heron Quays, London E14 4JP
www.octopusbooksusa.com

Distributed in the U.S. and Canada by Octopus Books USA:
c/o Hachette Book Group
237 Park Avenue
New York NY 10017

ISBN 978-0-600-61947-5

A CIP catalog record for this book is available from the Library
of Congress.

Printed and bound in China

1 2 3 4 5 6 7 8 9 10

For Rosalind, wonderfully hospitable but
a very last-minute cook. Perhaps this will help!

Standard level spoon measurements are used in all recipes.

Ovens should be preheated to the specified temperature
—if using a fan-assisted oven, follow the manufacturer's
instructions for adjusting the time and the temperature.

Fresh herbs should be used unless otherwise stated.

Medium eggs should be used unless otherwise stated.

The Food and Drug Administration advises that eggs should
not be consumed raw. This book contains some dishes made
with raw or lightly cooked eggs. It is prudent for vulnerable
people such as pregnant and nursing mothers, invalids, the
elderly, babies, and young children to avoid uncooked or lightly
cooked dishes made with eggs. Once prepared, these dishes
should be kept refrigerated and used promptly.

This book includes dishes made with nuts and nut derivatives.
It is advisable for those with known allergic reactions to nuts
and nut derivatives and those who may be potentially
vulnerable to these allergies, such as pregnant and nursing
mothers, invalids, the elderly, babies, and children, to avoid
dishes made with nuts and nut oils. It is also prudent to check
the labels of pre-prepared ingredients for the possible inclusion
of nut derivatives.

Finishing time refers to how long it will take you to complete the
dish when ready to serve.

contents

introduction

introduction

We all lead such busy lives nowadays that any method for reducing stress should be welcomed. Finding time to make a healthy and enjoyable meal for the family, or something special for friends, can sometimes feel like another chore, but it needn't be. Making food in advance ready to bake later in the day may sound a little old fashioned, but don't discount it.

While no one is suggesting that you knock up a fish pie before getting the 8.03 train to work, part-making dishes at the weekend leaves you free to indulge in a little retail therapy, a trip to the gym, or a long walk with the dog. Then when you return you can sit

down and relax with a drink while supper reheats, filling the house with all its wonderful aromas.

Making food to share with friends is also much more relaxing when you have done most of the work earlier in the day. When your guests arrive you can enjoy their company, rather than spending all your time in the kitchen.

For those with young families, supper can be started while very young children have a morning nap or are at school, then when you feel at your most tired you have time for a cuddle and a story while supper cooks. If you work shifts, making food earlier in the day, or even the evening before, is also a boon as supper can be left with a note so that the first home pops it in the oven, ready for everyone to tuck into the minute they walk in.

If you are newly retired, it can be liberating to make supper early in the day then go out and enjoy your long-awaited free time and eat whenever you feel like it, so maximizing your time on the golf course or in pursuit of new hobbies. Or why not go out for the day with a gourmet picnic lunch, such as a raised pork and chicken Picnic Pie, or Pan Bagna.

This book contains an eclectic selection of traditional and modern recipes, with something to suit all moods and occasions, to help you get one step ahead.

make ahead hints & tips

be organized

The key to success when it comes to making meals in advance is to be organized. Plan what you are going to eat well in advance so you know which ingredients you need to buy, what you need to prepare, and when. If you have to, write it down so you don't forget.

choose the right dishes

Some dishes lend themselves to being made in advance. Moist dishes that cook for a long time, such as curries, casseroles, and soups, are often even better when made in advance and reheated as the flavors get a chance to really develop. Or choose mousses, salads, sushi, or desserts which are served cold and can be kept chilled until you want to eat them. With these dishes you have nothing at all to do just before serving, making them perfect for entertaining. Other dishes, such as pies or kebabs, can be part-made in advance, then simply baked or broiled at the last minute.

frozen assets

It may sound a little old fashioned, but the freezer can be a great help to the busy cook. A few well-chosen supplies can be quickly transformed into an easy dessert. Frozen fruits such as raspberries, blackberries, blueberries, and cranberries look just as good

when defrosted as fresh and make pretty accompaniments to desserts such as crème caramel or even a good-quality ice cream, or as the base for a warming crumble. Packs of frozen puff, shortcrust, and phyllo pastry save greatly on time and effort—think sweet as well as savory pies. Don't throw those stale bits of bread away, but make into crumbs and freeze ready for sprinkling onto cheesy gratin dishes or mixing into stuffings.

get planting

Don't forget a few pots of fresh herbs by the front or back door. Herbs not only look pretty but can save money too and mean that you always have a handy supply for a garnish or extra flavor whenever you need it.

food hygiene

When cooking meals in advance, food hygiene becomes extremely important. If food is wrongly stored, handled, or reheated, harmful bacteria can multiply and eventually cause food poisoning. Follow these simple guidelines to make sure your food is safe.

cover ups

Once food is prepared and ready to be set aside for later it is important to cover dishes to prevent food from drying out. Use either kitchen foil, plastic wrap, or, if chilling in the dish it was cooked in, the casserole or saucepan lid. Choose kitchen foil or the dish lid if the food will be reheated, covered, in the oven. Use plastic wrap for salads or oven-baked dishes that are cooked uncovered for a golden crust.

cooling

Once food has been cooked, cover it and allow it to cool to room temperature. As soon as it is cool enough, transfer it to the refrigerator until required.

Speed up the cooling of meat dishes such as casseroles or pâtés by standing the covered cooking dish in a sink or roasting pan filled with cold water.

refrigerator reminders

- The bottom of the refrigerator is the coldest part as cold air falls.
- Always cover food, either raw or cooked, before putting it in the refrigerator. This not only prevents food from drying out but also helps to prevent strong flavors, particularly garlicky or spicy ones, from transferring.
- Keep cooked and uncooked foods on separate shelves to prevent contamination, with uncooked foods on the lower shelves.
- Make sure that meat or fish juices—which are high in bacteria—cannot drip onto other foods, particularly those that will be eaten raw such as salad or cheese.
- Never put warm dishes in the refrigerator.
- Do not overcrowd the refrigerator or the cold air will not be able to circulate freely.
- Keep the times that the refrigerator door is open to a minimum to maintain a safe temperature and save energy.

listeria

There is only a small risk of a healthy person contracting listeriosis. It is recommended that those most at risk, such as the elderly, pregnant mothers, or those recovering from illness, avoid foods which have been found to contain high levels of listeria bacteria as these can continue to multiply at refrigerator temperatures. These foods include soft mold-ripened cheeses such as Brie, Camembert, and blue cheeses; meat, fish, or vegetable pâtés; and raw unpasteurized milk and milk products.

what temperature?

Refrigerators should be kept at a temperature of 32–41°F in the center to the lower shelves. You can buy a refrigerator thermometer from a hardware or kitchen store. You may need to reduce the temperature during summer.

reheating

Correct reheating of make ahead meals is as important as correct storage. There are three golden rules:
• Only reheat foods once.
• If you don't require the full amount reheated, then take a portion out and reheat so that the remaining portions may be reheated later.
• Always make sure that the food is piping hot right through before serving.

reheating on the stove

Make sure that food is brought to boiling point and then kept at that temperature for 5 minutes, stirring to make sure that it does not stick to the base of the pan.

reheating in the oven

Reheat food at 350°F, Gas Mark 4, or above for a minimum of 20 minutes or for longer if a large dish, until piping hot right through.

reheating in the microwave

Do not use metal dishes to reheat in the microwave, and beware of china dishes that have metal decoration as these will cause sparks while the microwave is in operation. Everyday china plates and bowls are fine, but be wary of pottery dishes as these can get as hot as the food, so use a cloth to remove items from the microwave.

Cover food with plastic wrap while reheating to prevent it from splattering all over the microwave interior. Pierce the plastic wrap once or twice to allow the steam to escape.

Reheat dishes thoroughly, rather than to the point that it is just hot enough to eat. Food must be heated until piping hot throughout, ideally held at 158°F for 2 minutes.

Always stir foods before serving to disperse any hot spots.

appetizers

smoked salmon & shrimp sushi

Preparation time **40 minutes**
Cooking time **20–25 minutes**
Finishing time **5 minutes**
Serves **4–6**

1¾ cups **water**
1¼ cups **sushi rice**
4 tablespoons **rice vinegar**
1 teaspoon **wasabi paste**,
  plus extra to serve
8 oz cooked **jumbo shrimp**
grated zest and juice of
  2 **limes**
5 sheets **nori seaweed**
7 oz sliced **smoked salmon**
1½ oz bottled Japanese
  ginger, drained
11 oz jar of **red pimentos**,
  drained and cut into long
  strips
3 **scallions**, cut into long
  thin strips

Bring the water to a boil in a saucepan, add the rice, cover, and simmer gently for 20–25 minutes until very soft. Drain off any excess water. Mix the vinegar and wasabi and stir into the rice. Let cool. Toss the shrimp with the lime zest and juice and set aside.

Place one nori sheet on a bamboo rolling mat, spoon over one-fifth of the rice, and spread into an even layer, leaving a small border of nori showing. Arrange one-fifth of the smoked salmon in a long line in the center of the rice. Next to that add one-fifth of the shrimp, and on top some ginger, pimentos, and scallions.

Using the mat to help, roll up the nori sheet so the rice wraps around the filling and the edges of nori overlap slightly. Rock back and forth for an even shape. Repeat to make the remaining rolls. Wrap them individually in plastic wrap and chill until required.

When ready to serve, cut the rolls into thick slices and arrange with cut edges uppermost on a plate. Serve with extra wasabi.

For fennel & asparagus sushi, cut a fennel bulb into strips and blanch in boiling water with 5 oz asparagus for 2 minutes until just tender. Refresh the vegetables in cold water, then drain and pat dry with paper towels. Use the fennel and asparagus in place of the smoked salmon and shrimp.

cherry tomato tarts with pesto

Preparation time **15 minutes**
Finishing time **18 minutes**
Serves **4**

12 oz cherry **tomatoes**
2 tablespoons **olive oil**
1 **onion**, finely chopped
2 **garlic cloves**, crushed
3 tablespoons **sundried
   tomato paste**
11 oz ready-made **puff pastry**
beaten **egg**, to glaze
⅔ cup **sour cream**
2 tablespoons **pesto**
salt and **pepper**

Lightly grease a large baking sheet and sprinkle with water. Halve about 10 of the tomatoes. Heat the oil in a skillet, add the onion, and fry for about 3 minutes until softened. Remove the pan from the heat, add the garlic and sundried tomato paste, then stir in all the tomatoes, turning until they are lightly coated in the sauce. Chill and set aside until required.

Roll out the pastry on a lightly floured surface and cut out four 5 inch rounds using a cutter or small bowl as a guide. Transfer to the prepared baking sheet and make a shallow cut ½ inch in from the edge of each round using the tip of a sharp knife, to form a rim. Brush the rims with beaten egg. Cover, chill, and set aside until required.

Lightly mix together the sour cream, pesto, and salt and pepper in a bowl so that the sour cream is streaked with the pesto. Cover, chill, and set aside until required.

When ready to serve, pile the tomato mixture onto the centers of the pastries, making sure the mixture stays within the rims. Bake the tartlets in a preheated oven, 425°F, for about 15 minutes until the pastry is risen and golden. Transfer the tartlets to serving plates and spoon the sour cream and pesto mixture into a small serving dish. Serve sprinkled with basil leaves.

For homemade pesto, put 1 chopped garlic clove, a large handful of basil leaves, 3 tablespoons pine nuts, and ½ cup grated Parmesan cheese in a food processor or blender and process, gradually adding a little olive oil to make a thick, oily paste.

gravadlax with dill sauce

Preparation time **10 minutes**, plus **2–3 days** marinating
Finishing time **15 minutes**
Serves **4–6**

large handful of **dill weed**
1 tablespoon **mixed peppercorns**, roughly crushed
2 tablespoons **salt flakes**
2 tablespoons **light brown sugar**
1 lb piece of thick **salmon** fillet, skinned

Dill sauce
2 tablespoons **Swedish** or **Dijon mustard**
4 teaspoons **light brown sugar**
3 tablespoons **sunflower oil**
1–2 teaspoons **white wine vinegar**
2 tablespoons chopped **dill weed**
pepper

Tear half the dill into pieces onto a plate. Add the peppercorns, salt, and sugar and mix together. Coat both sides of the salmon in the dill mixture then transfer to a large strong plastic bag with any mixture from the plate. Seal the bag and stand in a shallow dish. Cover with a cutting board and weigh down with an unopened bag of flour, bags of sugar, or cans. Marinate in the refrigerator for 2–3 days, turning twice a day.

On the day of serving, make the sauce by mixing the mustard and sugar together in a small bowl. Gradually trickle in the oil, little by little, whisking continuously until thickened. Thin the sauce with vinegar to taste. Stir in the chopped dill and season with pepper.

When ready to serve, lift the salmon out of the marinade, drain, put on a cutting board. Sprinkle with the remaining dill, torn into pieces. Cut into thin slices with the knife at a 45 degree angle to the fish. Arrange on serving plates with spoonfuls of the sauce and a little salad garnish. Serve with brown bread.

For honeyed gravadlax with fennel & dill, add 1 teaspoon roughly crushed fennel seeds to the marinade mixture, and use 2 tablespoons thick honey instead of the sugar. Serve in the same way, accompanied by dill sauce and brown bread.

spring rolls

Preparation time **20 minutes**, plus soaking

Finishing time **about 40 minutes**

Makes **40**

2 oz thin **cellophane** (bean thread) **noodles**

½ oz dried **black ear fungus**

4 oz ground **pork**

2 **shallots**, chopped

3 **garlic cloves**, crushed

1 inch piece of fresh **ginger root**, peeled and finely chopped

½ tablespoon **soy sauce**

10 round **rice papers**

2 **eggs**, beaten

peanut oil, for deep-frying

ground black **pepper**

Soak the noodles and fungus in separate bowls of warm water for 20 minutes or until they are soft.

Use scissors to snip the noodles into 1 inch lengths and chop the fungus into small pieces. Mix together with the pork, shallots, garlic, ginger, soy sauce, and pepper.

Cut each round of rice paper into 4 quarters. Brush each quarter with egg and allow to soften for a couple of minutes. Place 1 heaping teaspoon of filling toward the rounded edge of the rice paper, fold in the sides, and roll up toward the pointed end. Repeat with the remaining filling and rice paper. Cover and chill the rolls until required.

When ready to serve, heat the oil for deep-frying in a saucepan until a cube of bread browns in 2 minutes. Add about 6 spring rolls and cook for 6–8 minutes or until they are golden brown and the filling cooked through. Repeat with the remaining spring rolls and serve immediately with sweet chili dipping sauce.

For shrimp spring rolls, prepare the noodles, garlic, and ginger as above. Mix with 1¼ cups bean sprouts, 1 small grated carrot, 3 sliced scallions, 2 tablespoons chopped cilantro, 5 oz cooked peeled shrimp, and 2 teaspoons Thai fish sauce. Separate the rice papers but leave whole. Brush with egg, divide the filling between them, then fold in the sides and roll up. Cook as above.

chickpea & parsley soup

Preparation time **15 minutes**, plus soaking
Cooking time **1½–2 hours**
Finishing time **5 minutes**
Serves **4–6**

1½ cups dried **chickpeas**, soaked overnight
1 small **onion**, quartered
3 **garlic cloves**
¾ cup **parsley**
2 tablespoons **olive oil**
5 cups **vegetable stock**
finely grated zest and juice of ½ **lemon**
salt and **pepper**

Drain the chickpeas, rinse in cold water, and drain again. Put them in a saucepan of fresh water, bring to a boil, boil rapidly for 10 minutes then simmer for 1–1½ hours, until just tender.

Put the onion, garlic, and parsley in a food processor or blender and blend until finely chopped. Heat the oil in a large saucepan and cook the onion mixture over a low heat until slightly softened.

Add the chickpeas and cook gently for 1–2 minutes. Add the stock, season well with salt and pepper, and bring to a boil. Cover and cook for 20 minutes, or until the chickpeas are really tender.

Allow the soup to cool a little, then part-puree it in a food processor or blender, or mash it with a fork, so that it retains plenty of texture. Cover and chill until required.

When ready to serve, pour the soup into a clean pan, add the lemon juice, adjust the seasoning as necessary and heat through. Serve the soup topped with grated lemon zest and cracked black pepper.

For lentil & cilantro soup, cook 1¼ cups red lentils in a covered saucepan with 4 cups gently simmering water for 30 minutes until just tender. Process 1 onion, 1 large mild seeded red chili, 3 garlic cloves, 1 tablespoon curry paste, and 1½ cups cilantro in a blender, fry as above, and stir into the lentils with 1¼ cups extra stock. Season and cook, uncovered, for 10 minutes. Allow to cool. Reheat when ready to serve.

roasted garlic & celeriac soup

Preparation time **25 minutes**
Cooking time **45 minutes**
Finishing time **5 minutes**
Serves **4**

2 small heads of **garlic**, halved
3 teaspoons **olive oil**
2 tablespoons **butter**
1 lb **celeriac**, peeled and cut into chunks
1 **onion**, roughly chopped
4 cups **vegetable stock**
⅔ cup **milk**
1½ oz sliced **pancetta**
⅔ cup **light cream**
salt and **pepper**

Put the halved unpeeled garlic heads into a small roasting pan, drizzle with 1 teaspoon of the oil and roast in a preheated oven, 400°F, for 15 minutes. Meanwhile, heat the remaining oil and the butter in a saucepan, add the celeriac and onion, cover, and fry gently for 10 minutes, shaking the pan from time to time.

Take the garlic out of its paper skins with the tip of a small knife and add to the celeriac. Pour in the stock, add a little seasoning, and bring to a boil. Cover and simmer for 30 minutes, or until the celeriac is tender. Cool slightly.

Puree the soup in batches in a food processor or blender then pour back into the pan. Cool completely then chill until required.

When ready to serve, stir the milk into the soup and reheat until piping hot. Dry fry the pancetta until crisp and golden and cut into long thin strips. Stir half the cream into the soup then ladle into serving bowls. Swirl the remaining cream into the soup. Sprinkle the soup with the pancetta and serve immediately.

For roasted garlic & pumpkin soup, use 1 lb seeded pumpkin. Peel and chop, then use the pumpkin instead of the celeriac. Garnish with cream as above, adding toasted pumpkin seeds instead of pancetta.

black bean soup with noodles

Preparation time **15 minutes**
Finishing time **10 minutes**
Serves **4**

2 tablespoons **peanut** or
  vegetable oil
bunch of **scallions**, sliced
2 **garlic cloves**, roughly
  chopped
1 **red chili**, seeded and sliced
1½ inch piece of fresh **ginger
  root**, peeled and grated
½ cup **black bean sauce**
3 cups **vegetable stock**
3½ cups **bok choy** or **collard
  greens**, shredded
2 teaspoons **soy sauce**
1 teaspoon **superfine sugar**
¼ cup raw, unsalted shelled
  peanuts
7 oz dried **soba noodles**,
  cooked

Prepare all the vegetables in advance. When ready to
serve, heat the oil in a saucepan. Add the scallions and
garlic and fry gently for 1 minute. Add the chili, ginger,
black bean sauce, and stock and bring to a boil.

Stir in the bok choy or collard greens, soy sauce, sugar,
and peanuts, reduce the heat, and simmer gently,
uncovered, for 4 minutes.

Pile the cooked noodles into four serving bowls. Ladle
the soup over the noodles and serve immediately.

For miso broth with shrimp & noodles, fry the
scallions and garlic as above. Add the chili, ginger,
and fish stock instead of the vegetable stock,
2 tablespoons miso, 2 tablespoons mirin, soy, and
sugar as above. Cook for 5 minutes and allow to
cool. Finish with 1¾ cups bok choy, 5 oz cooked
shrimp, and 5 oz cooked soba noodles.

tomato soup with tio pepe

Preparation time **25 minutes**
Cooking time **30 minutes**
Finishing time **5 minutes**
Serves **4**

1 lb plum **tomatoes**, halved
2 tablespoons **olive oil**
1 **onion**, roughly chopped
½ teaspoon **smoked paprika**
1 cup **sundried tomatoes** in
  oil, drained and roughly
  chopped
1¾ cups **vegetable stock**
2–3 tablespoons **Tio Pepe**
  dry **sherry**
1 teaspoon **superfine sugar**
salt and **pepper**

Croutons
4 tablespoons **olive oil**
¼ teaspoon **smoked paprika**
4 oz rustic **white bread**,
  cubed

Put the tomatoes, cut sides up, in the base of a broiler pan, drizzle with 1 tablespoon of the oil, season, and cook under a preheated hot broiler for 5 minutes until browned. Heat the remaining oil in a saucepan, add the onion, and fry for 5 minutes until pale golden. Stir in the paprika and cook for 1 minute. Add the broiled tomatoes and crush with a wooden spoon, then mix in the sundried tomatoes, stock, sherry, and sugar, and season to taste with salt and pepper. Bring to a boil then cover and simmer for 20 minutes.

Meanwhile, make the croutons. Mix the oil and paprika together in a plastic bag, add the cubed bread, and toss together. Tip out onto a baking sheet and cook in a preheated oven, 400°F, for 10 minutes or until crisp and golden.

Cool the soup slightly then puree in batches in a blender or food processor until smooth. Sieve and return to the saucepan, cover, and set aside until required. When ready to serve, reheat the soup until piping hot, ladle into small bowls, and sprinkle with the croutons and a little olive oil.

For roasted red pepper soup with Tio Pepe, omit the tomatoes. Fry 1 chopped onion and mix in ½ teaspoon paprika as above. Drain and chop the peppers from a 1½ lb jar of roasted peppers and mix with 1 cup sundried tomatoes. Finish as above.

broccoli & cheddar soup

Preparation time **10 minutes**
Cooking time **30 minutes**
Finishing time **5 minutes**
Serves **6**

2 lb **broccoli**
¼ cup **butter**
1 **onion**, chopped
1 large **potato**, peeled
  and quartered
6 cups **vegetable stock**
½ cup **light cream**
1 tablespoon **lemon juice**
1 teaspoon **Worcestershire
  sauce**
a few drops of **Tabasco
  sauce**
1 cup grated sharp **cheddar
  cheese**
salt and **pepper**

Remove all the tough stems and leaves from the broccoli. Cut off the stalks, peel them, and cut them into 1 inch pieces. Break the florets into very small pieces and set them aside.

Melt the butter in a large saucepan. Add the onion and broccoli stalks and cook, covered, for 5 minutes over a medium heat, stirring frequently.

Add the broccoli florets, potato, and vegetable stock to the pan. Bring the mixture to a boil and cook, partially covered, for 5 minutes. Using a slotted spoon, remove 6 or more florets for a garnish and set aside. Season the mixture with salt and pepper and continue to cook for 20 minutes, or until all the vegetables are soft.

Using a blender or food processor, puree the mixture in batches until smooth, transferring each successive batch to a clean saucepan. Chill until required.

When ready to serve, add the cream, lemon juice, Worcestershire sauce, and a few drops of Tabasco to the pan. Heat the soup gently and simmer for 3–5 minutes, but do not allow the soup to boil. Just before serving, stir in the grated cheese. Serve the soup, garnished with the reserved broccoli or watercress, if desired.

For creamy cauliflower & cheddar soup, cut 1 large cauliflower into small florets. Fry in 2 tablespoons butter and 1 tablespoon olive oil with 1 chopped onion as above. Add 2½ cups vegetable stock, season, and simmer for 10 minutes. Puree in batches, return to the pan. Chill until required. Stir in 1¾ cups milk, 2 teaspoons Dijon mustard, and a little grated nutmeg. Reheat and stir in ¾ cup grated cheddar.

fish mousse with walnut salad

Preparation time **20 minutes**
Cooking time **3–4 minutes**
Finishing time **5 minutes**
Serves **4**

5 oz sliced **cold-smoked
     rainbow trout** or **smoked
     salmon**
6 tablespoons full-fat **sour
     cream**
finely grated zest of ½ **lemon**
1 tablespoon **lemon juice**
6 oz mixed **hot-smoked fish**
     (trout, salmon, and
     mackerel fillet)
salt and **pepper**

Salad
3 tablespoons **walnut pieces**
3 tablespoons **olive oil**
1 tablespoon **red wine
     vinegar**
1 cup **watercress**

Line 4⅔ cup pudding molds or china ramekin dishes with plastic wrap, then line the bases and sides with the sliced trout, keeping a little back for putting on the tops.

Mix the sour cream, lemon zest, and lemon juice with a little black pepper. Flake the fish, discarding any skin and bones, then fold it into the sour cream mixture. Divide between the lined molds then cover with the remaining sliced trout. Fold any overhanging pieces of trout over the top then chill until required.

To make the salad dressing, toast the walnuts in a dry skillet over a medium heat until lightly browned. Mix the oil, vinegar, and a little seasoning together then add to the hot walnuts and set aside.

When ready to serve, tear any very long stems off the watercress then toss with the dressing. Unmold the mousses, remove the plastic wrap, and arrange on 4 small plates. Spoon the salad around and serve with warmed crusty brown rolls, if desired.

For smoked fish toasts with walnut salad, omit the cold smoked rainbow trout. Make the sour cream, lemon, and hot smoked fish mix as above. Spread onto toasted slices of thin whole-wheat baguette. Serve with salad leaves tossed in lemon juice as above.

broiled eggplant parcels

Preparation time **15 minutes**
Cooking time **2 minutes**
Finishing time **10 minutes**
Serves **4**

1 long, large **eggplant**
4 oz **mozzarella cheese**
1 large or 2 small plum
   tomatoes
8 large **basil** leaves
1 tablespoon **olive oil**
1 tablespoon **pine nuts**,
   dry-fried in a hot pan
   until golden
salt and **pepper**

Tomato dressing
2 tablespoons **olive oil**
1 teaspoon **balsamic vinegar**
1 teaspoon **sundried tomato**
   paste
1 teaspoon **lemon juice**

Remove the stalk from the eggplant and cut it lengthwise into 8 slices, disregarding the 2 outer edges. Put the eggplant slices in a pan of boiling salted water and cook for 2 minutes, then drain and dry on paper towels. Cut the mozzarella into 4 slices and the tomato into 8 slices, disregarding the outer edges.

Place 2 of the eggplant slices in a flameproof dish, forming a cross. Place a slice of tomato on top, season with salt and pepper, add a basil leaf, a slice of mozzarella, another basil leaf, then more salt and pepper, and finally another slice of tomato. Fold the edges of the eggplant around the filling. Repeat with the other ingredients to make 4 parcels in total. Cover and chill for 20 minutes, or until required.

To make the dressing, beat together the oil, vinegar, tomato paste, and lemon juice. Cover and set aside until required.

When ready to serve, brush the eggplant parcels with olive oil. Place the dish under a preheated hot broiler and cook for about 5 minutes on each side, until golden brown. Serve hot, drizzled with the dressing and sprinkled with the pine nuts and extra basil leaves.

For eggplant & tomato salad, drain a 7 oz chilled carton roasted eggplant and red sweet peppers, reserving the oil. Arrange in a dish with 4 sliced plum tomatoes, 8 oz drained, sliced mozzarella, a small bunch of torn basil leaves, and a few black olives. Make the dressing by mixing 3 tablespoons of the reserved oil, 1 tablespoon red wine vinegar, and 1 finely chopped garlic clove and season.

potted crab & shrimp

Preparation time **20 minutes**, plus chilling
Cooking time **10 minutes**
Finishing time **5 minutes**
Serves **4**

1 cup **butter**, diced
finely grated zest and juice of 1 **lime**
3 tablespoons chopped **cilantro**
generous pinch of **cayenne pepper**
7 oz peeled, cooked **shrimp**, roughly chopped
1 dressed **crab**, about 6 oz
½ small **whole-wheat baguette**, sliced
2 heads of **Belgian endive**
a few tiny **radishes**
salt

First clarify the butter. Heat a small saucepan of water, add the butter, and heat gently until melted. Cool, then freeze until the butter has formed a set layer on top of the water. Lift the disk of hardened butter off the water and discard the water. Remove any droplets of water from the underside of the butter with paper towels.

Melt half the clarified butter in a saucepan. Add the lime zest, chopped cilantro, cayenne, and a little salt. Stir the shrimp into the butter with the crabmeat and lime juice. Heat until piping hot. Spoon into 4 small china ramekins and press down well so there are no air pockets. Chill for 15 minutes.

Melt the remaining butter in a clean pan then spoon over the top of the fish mixture in a thin even layer. Chill for 3–4 hours until set. Sprinkle with a little extra cayenne.

When ready to serve, toast the bread then arrange on plates with the dishes of potted fish. Serve with Belgian endive leaves and tiny radishes.

For potted shrimp with chives, use chopped chives instead of the cilantro. Replace the lime zest and juice with the finely grated zest of 1 lemon and 2 tablespoons lemon juice. Use 12 oz shrimp in place of the crab and shrimp.

chicken satay

Preparation time **10 minutes**, plus marinating
Finishing time **10 minutes**
Serves **6**

2 tablespoons smooth **peanut butter**
½ cup **soy sauce**
½ cup **lime juice**
2–3 tablespoons **curry powder**
2 **garlic cloves**, chopped
1 teaspoon **hot pepper sauce**
6 skinless **chicken breast fillets**, cubed

Combine the peanut butter, soy sauce, lime juice, curry powder, garlic, and hot pepper sauce in a nonmetallic dish. Add the chicken, mix well, and chill for 12 hours or until required.

When ready to serve, divide the chicken cubes between 6 metal skewers and cook under a preheated hot broiler for 5 minutes on each side until tender and cooked through. Serve immediately with lemon wedges and chunks of cucumber and onion, if desired.

For miso-broiled chicken, mix 2 tablespoons each soy sauce, dry sherry or rice wine, and 2 teaspoons honey and miso paste. Add the cubed chicken and marinate as above. Thread onto skewers and cook as above. Serve with rice and a sliced cucumber and red chili salad.

black olive tapenade toasts

Preparation time **15 minutes**
Cooking time **3–4 minutes**
Finishing time **10 minutes**
Serves **4**

12 slices of thin **baguette**
1 **garlic clove**, halved
1 cup marinated, pitted mixed
  olives
2 tablespoons **olive oil**
small bunch of **basil**
¼ cup grated **pecorino** or
  Parmesan cheese

Toast the bread lightly on both sides then rub one side with the garlic. Transfer to a baking sheet.

Finely chop the olives in a blender or food processor, then add the oil and most of the basil and blend again to make a coarse paste. Spread over the garlic toasts. Cover loosely and chill until required.

When ready to serve, remove the cover and cook the toasts in a preheated oven, 375°F, for 10 minutes. Arrange on a serving plate and sprinkle with the pecorino or Parmesan and the remaining basil leaves.

For fava bean tapenade toasts, fry ½ chopped onion and 1 finely chopped garlic clove in 1 tablespoon olive oil for 5 minutes until softened. Add 1¼ cups frozen fava beans and 5 tablespoons vegetable stock, then simmer for 5 minutes. Mash or process until a coarse paste, stir in 2 tablespoons lemon juice, a small bunch of chopped parsley or cilantro, and salt and pepper. When ready to serve, toast 4 pita breads, tear into strips, and top with bean paste. Garnish with extra herbs.

fresh fava bean & chili dip

Preparation time **5 minutes**
Cooking time **10 minutes**
Finishing time **5 minutes**
Serves **4**

2¼ cups fresh or frozen **fava beans**
1 cup **parsley**, coarsely chopped
3 cups **cilantro**, coarsely chopped
1–2 mild **green chilies**, seeded and chopped
2 **garlic cloves**, chopped
1½ teaspoons ground **cumin**
3 tablespoons **olive oil**
1 **onion**, thinly sliced
salt

Cook the beans in a pan of boiling salted water for 5 minutes. Add the herbs, cover, and simmer for an additional 5 minutes. Drain, reserving some of the cooking liquid.

Place the cooked beans in a blender or food processor with the chilies, garlic, cumin, 2 tablespoons of the oil, and 3–4 tablespoons of the reserved cooking liquid. Process to a smooth paste, season to taste, and add a little more cooking liquid if it is too dry. Transfer to a serving dish and chill until required.

When ready to serve, heat the remaining oil in a non-stick skillet and fry the onion briskly until golden and crisp. Spread over the dip and serve with crudites or whole-wheat pita breads.

For avocado & chili dip, drain 13½ oz can chickpeas and put in a blender with 2 tablespoons toasted sesame seeds, 1 mild seeded red chili, 4 tablespoons lemon juice, 2 finely chopped garlic cloves, 6 tablespoons plain yogurt, and seasoning. Blend until smooth then set aside. When ready to serve, add the flesh of 1 avocado and blend again. Serve with warm pita breads.

mini bacon, prune, & stilton grills

Preparation time **15 minutes**
Finishing time **10–15 minutes**
Serves **4**

3 oz **Stilton cheese**, rind
    removed
16 large pitted ready-to-eat
    prunes
8 slices of **bacon**
1½ tablespoons **butter**
4 slices of **bread**

Cut the cheese into 16 squares, make a slit in each prune then insert a cube of cheese. Cut each slice of bacon in half and wrap one half around each stuffed prune.

Lightly butter the slices of bread, cut each into 4 squares, and arrange on a baking sheet. Place one prune on the top of each piece of bread, then secure in place with a toothpick. Cover and chill until required.

When ready to serve, remove the cover and bake in a preheated oven, 400°F, for 10–15 minutes until the bread and bacon are crisp and golden and the cheese just melted. Arrange on one large serving plate or individual plates, garnished with arugula.

For angels on horseback, wrap 16 shelled oysters in halved bacon slices and hold in place with toothpicks. Grill the bacon-wrapped oysters and squares of buttered bread separately until just cooked, then assemble and serve immediately.

nut koftas with minted yogurt

Preparation time **15 minutes**
Cooking time **5 minutes**
Finishing time **10 minutes**
Serves **4**

6 tablespoons **vegetable oil**
1 **onion**, chopped
½ teaspoon **dried red pepper flakes**
2 **garlic cloves**, roughly chopped
1 tablespoon medium **curry paste**
14 oz can **cranberry** or **cannellini beans**, rinsed and drained
1 cup **ground almonds**
½ cup salted **almonds**, chopped
1 small **egg**
¾ cup **Greek** or **whole milk yogurt**
2 tablespoons chopped **mint**
1 tablespoon **lemon juice**
8 mini **naan breads**
salt and **pepper**

Heat 3 tablespoons of the oil in a skillet, add the onion and fry for 4 minutes. Add the pepper flakes, garlic, and curry paste and fry for 1 minute.

Transfer to a food processor or blender with the beans, ground almonds, salted almonds, egg, and a little salt and pepper and process until the mixture starts to bind together.

Using lightly floured hands, take about one-eighth of the mixture and mold it around a metal skewer, forming it into a sausage about 1 inch thick. Make 7 more koftas in the same way. Cover and chill until required.

Mix together the yogurt and mint in a small serving bowl and season to taste with salt and pepper. In a separate bowl, mix together 2 tablespoons oil, lemon juice, and a little salt and pepper. Cover both bowls and chill until required.

When ready to serve, place the koftas on a foil-lined broiler rack and brush with 1 tablespoon of oil. Cook under a preheated moderate broiler for about 5 minutes until golden, turning once. Brush the koftas with the lemon dressing and serve in warm naan breads, drizzled with the yogurt dressing.

For spiced lamb koftas, mix 1 lb ground lamb with 4 finely chopped scallions and 1 teaspoon each ground cumin and ground coriander. Season well, shape into small balls, and chill until required. Thread onto metal skewers and broil for about 10 minutes, turning until cooked through. Serve with yogurt and naan breads as above.

marinated shrimp skewers

Preparation time **20 minutes**
Finishing time **7–8 minutes**
Serves **4**

13 oz raw **jumbo shrimp** in
  their shells
finely grated zest and juice
  of 1 **lemon**
finely grated zest and juice
  of 1 **lime**
1 tablespoon **sesame oil**
2 **garlic** cloves, finely chopped
salt and **pepper**

Pickled cucumber salad
½ **cucumber**
¼–½ mild **red chili**, seeded
  and finely chopped
2 tablespoons chopped
  cilantro
1 tablespoon **white wine**
  vinegar
1 teaspoon **Thai fish sauce**
½ teaspoon **superfine sugar**
fresh **cilantro** and **lime**
  wedges to garnish, optional

Divide the shrimp between 8 wooden skewers. In a shallow ceramic dish long enough to hold the skewers, beat together the grated zest and juice of the lemon and lime, the oil, and garlic. Season with salt and pepper, add the shrimp skewers, and coat in the marinade. Cover and chill until required.

Very thinly slice the cucumber and put into a shallow dish. Sprinkle with the chili, cilantro, vinegar, fish sauce, and sugar. Cover and chill until required.

When ready to serve, place the skewers under a preheated hot broiler with the exposed parts of the skewers away from the heat. Cook for 7–8 minutes, turning once, until the shrimp are bright pink all over. Stir the salad and spoon into small bowls set on plates. Add two skewers to each plate, and garnish with cilantro sprigs and lime wedges, if desired.

For marinated beef skewers, cut 1¼ lb sirloin steak into cubes, then thread onto skewers and marinate in 3 tablespoons good-quality bought teriyaki marinade and the grated zest and juice of 1 lime. Broil as above and serve with a pickled cucumber salad.

eggplant pâté

Preparation time **10 minutes**, plus soaking
Cooking time **15 minutes**
Serves **6**

⅔ cup dried **porcini mushrooms**
6 tablespoons **olive oil**
1 lb **eggplants**, cut into ½ inch dice
1 small **red onion**, chopped
2 teaspoons **cumin seeds**
6 oz **chestnut mushrooms**
2 **garlic cloves**, crushed
3 **pickled walnuts**, halved
small handful of **cilantro**
salt and **pepper**

Place the dried mushrooms in a bowl and cover with boiling water. Leave to soak for 10 minutes.

Meanwhile, heat the oil in a large skillet. Add the eggplants and onion and fry gently for 8 minutes until the vegetables are softened and browned.

Drain the dried mushrooms and add to the pan with the cumin seeds, fresh mushrooms, and garlic. Fry for an additional 5–7 minutes until the eggplants are very soft.

Transfer the mixture to a food processor or blender with the pickled walnuts and cilantro, season to taste with salt and pepper, and process until broken up but not completely smooth. Transfer to a serving dish and chill until required. Serve the pâté on thick slices of bread or hot toast.

For mushroom chakchouka, make as above, adding the mushroom soaking liquid and 13 oz canned chopped tomatoes to the pan with the dried and fresh mushrooms. Cover and simmer for 15 minutes, then allow to cool. Reheat when needed. Serve with warm pita breads, and top each portion with a poached egg and some fresh cilantro.

red pepper & munster tartlets

Preparation time **15 minutes**, plus chilling
Cooking time **15 minutes**
Finishing time **25–30 minutes**
Serves **4**

13 oz ready-made **shortcrust pastry**
1 tablespoon **vegetable oil**
1 tablespoon **butter**
1 **red onion**, finely chopped
⅔ cup **light cream**
2 **eggs**
2 **garlic cloves**, crushed
5 tablespoons snipped **chives**
1 small **red bell pepper**, roasted, peeled, and thinly sliced
3 oz **Munster cheese**, roughly chopped
salt and **pepper**

Roll out the pastry on a lightly floured surface and use to line four 4 inch tartlet pans. Prick the bases, line with circles of waxed paper, and fill with pie weights, then chill for 30 minutes.

Place the tartlets on a baking sheet and bake blind in a preheated oven, 375°F, for 8 minutes. Remove the paper and beans and bake for an additional 2–3 minutes, or until the shells are crisp and beginning to brown. Remove from the oven and set aside until required.

Heat the oil and butter in a pan and fry the red onion until caramelized. Set aside until required. Beat the cream, eggs, salt, and pepper together. Add the crushed garlic and chives, and chill the mixture until required.

When ready to serve, divide the onion and the roasted red pepper strips between the pastry shells. Pour over the cream and egg mixture and sprinkle the Munster on top. Cook the tartlets on the middle shelf of a preheated oven, 375°F, for 20–25 minutes, or until just cooked. Garnish with basil leaves and snipped chives, if desired.

For leek & Gruyère tarts, make the pastry shells as above. Fry 2 small thinly sliced leeks in oil and butter then divide them equally between the tart shells. Add the cream mixture as above and 3 oz grated Gruyère instead of the Munster.

aïoli with vegetable dippers

Preparation time **15 minutes**
Finishing time **3 minutes**
Serves **4**

3 **garlic cloves**
2 **egg yolks**
1 teaspoon **Dijon mustard**
1 cup **olive oil**
2 tablespoons **lemon juice**
salt and **pepper**

Dippers
4 oz baby **carrots**, scrubbed,
   halved
4 oz **asparagus tips**
3 oz **sugar snap peas**
1 **small crisphead lettuce**,
   leaves separated

Crush the garlic in a mortar and pestle with a little salt and pepper. Transfer to a large mixing bowl and add the egg yolks and mustard.

Beat the ingredients together with a balloon whisk or electric mixer until just mixed, then gradually trickle in the oil, drop by drop to begin with, until the mixture begins to thicken. Then continue with the oil in a very thin steady stream until about half has been added.

Thin the mayonnaise with a little lemon juice, then continue beating in the oil very gradually until very thick. Taste and add a little more lemon juice if you desire. Cover and chill until required.

Blanch the asparagus and sugar snaps in a saucepan of boiling water for 2 minutes. Drain and allow to cool. Put all of the vegetables into a plastic bag and chill with the aïoli until required.

When ready to serve, spoon the aïoli into a bowl and set onto a large platter. Arrange the vegetables around the bowl and serve.

Note: If the aïoli should "split" or separate while you are making it, don't panic. Put 1 egg yolk into a separate bowl and then very gradually beat the split mixture into the new egg yolk until smooth once more.

For green mayonnaise with dippers, omit the garlic and stir 1¼ cups watercress, very finely chopped, into the mayonnaise at the end. Serve with strips of pepper, breadsticks, or blanched asparagus.

caramelized brie

Preparation time **10 minutes**
Finishing time **20 minutes**,
plus standing
Serves **4**

13 oz ready-made **puff pastry**
1 small **egg**
1 tablespoon **milk**
pinch of **salt**
2 small wheels of **Brie cheese**

Divide the pastry into 4 and roll out each piece on a lightly floured surface to form a thin round, 2 inches larger than the cheeses.

Make an egg glaze by beating together the egg, milk, and salt in a small bowl. Place each cheese wheel in the middle of a pastry round. Brush the pastry around the cheese with a little of the egg glaze and then top each with a second pastry round. Press all around the edges of the pastry rounds to seal the pieces together well, then trim the excess pastry to give a 1 inch border.

Transfer the cheeses to a baking sheet. Brush the tops and sides with more of the egg glaze and score the tops with a sharp knife to form a pattern. Cut 2 small slits in each top to allow steam to escape. Chill until required.

When ready to serve, bake the cheeses in a preheated oven, 425°F, for 20 minutes until the pastry is puffed up and golden. Allow to stand for 10 minutes before garnishing with parsley and shredded beet.

For baked Brie with cranberries, unwrap the cheeses, line the boxes with nonstick parchment paper and replace the cheeses. Top each cheese with 1 tablespoon cranberry sauce and ¼ chopped red onion. When ready to serve, bake uncovered at 350°F, for 5–10 minutes until warmed and soft. Serve with apple slices, cucumber, celery, and breadstick dippers.

tortillas with eggplant yogurt

Preparation time **10 minutes**
Cooking time **10 minutes**
Serves **4**

4 tablespoons **olive oil**
1 **eggplant**, thinly sliced
small handful of **mint**,
   chopped
small handful of chopped
   parsley
2 tablespoons chopped
   chives
1 **green chili**, seeded and
   thinly sliced
¾ cup **Greek** or **whole milk
   yogurt**
2 tablespoons **mayonnaise**
2 large **tortillas**
3 inch length of **cucumber**,
   thinly sliced
salt, **pepper**, and **paprika**

Heat the oil in a skillet. Add the eggplant and fry for about 10 minutes until golden on both sides. Drain and set aside to cool.

Mix the herbs with the chili, yogurt, and mayonnaise in a bowl and season to taste with salt and pepper.

Arrange the fried eggplant slices over the tortillas and spread with the yogurt mixture. Arrange the cucumber slices on top. Roll up each tortilla, sprinkle with paprika, and cut into thick slices. Chill until required.

For mexican turkey tortillas, fry 10 oz ground turkey in 1 tablespoon sunflower oil for 10 minutes until lightly browned. Stir in 1 teaspoon roughly crushed cumin seeds, 1 teaspoon paprika, and ½ teaspoon chili powder. Cook for 5 minutes, then cover and chill. When ready to serve, reheat the turkey and divide between 8 warmed tortillas. Top with ¾ cup plain yogurt, ½ small shredded iceberg lettuce, 2 diced tomatoes, and some torn cilantro leaves. Roll up tightly and serve immediately.

salads & light lunches

lentil, chorizo, & scallop salad

Preparation time **10 minutes**
Cooking time **15–20 minutes**
Finishing time **5–6 minutes**
Serves **4**

1¼ cups **puy lentils**
2 **red bell peppers**, quartered,
 cored, and seeded
6 tablespoons **olive oil**
3 tablespoons **balsamic**
 vinegar
5 oz **chorizo**, thinly sliced
 or diced
12 oz **scallops**, rinsed and
 patted dry
2 cups **arugula** leaves
salt and **pepper**

Cook the lentils in a saucepan of simmering water for 15–20 minutes until just tender but still holding their shape. Drain the lentils, rinse in cold water, and drain again.

Meanwhile, arrange the peppers, cut sides down, on a piece of foil on a broiler rack, brush with 1 tablespoon of the oil and broil for 10–15 minutes until softened and lightly charred. Wrap in foil while hot. When cool enough to handle, remove the skins and slice the flesh.

Mix 4 tablespoons of the oil in a bowl with the vinegar and a little seasoning. Add the lentils and toss well, then stir in the pepper strips. Cover and set aside.

When ready to serve, heat the remaining 1 tablespoon of oil in a skillet, add the chorizo, and fry for 2 minutes. Add the scallops and cook for 3–4 minutes, turning once, until browned and just cooked. Divide the arugula leaves between 4 serving plates. Spoon the lentils on top, then add the chorizo and scallops and serve immediately.

For warm goat cheese & lentil salad, cook the lentils and peppers as above. Slice 6 oz goat cheese and arrange on the oiled foil on the broiler rack. Sprinkle with pepper, some torn rosemary leaves, and a drizzle of olive oil. Broil until just beginning to melt, then transfer to the top of the lentil salad.

hot haloumi with fattoush salad

Preparation time **10 minutes**
Finishing time **5 minutes**
Serves **4**

¼ cup finely sliced **red
  bell pepper**
¼ cup finely sliced **yellow
  bell pepper**
¼ cup chopped **cucumber**
½ cup finely chopped
  scallions
1 tablespoon chopped
  parsley
1 tablespoon chopped **mint**
1 tablespoon chopped
  cilantro
2 teaspoons **olive oil**
4 oz **haloumi cheese**,
  thickly sliced

Dressing
½ teaspoon crushed **garlic**
1 tablespoon **olive oil**
2 tablespoons **lemon juice**
salt and **pepper**

Put the red and yellow peppers, cucumber, scallions, parsley, mint, and cilantro in a bowl. Mix well, cover, and chill until required.

To make the dressing, mix the garlic with the oil and lemon juice and season with salt and pepper to taste. Set aside until required.

When ready to serve, pour the dressing over the salad and toss lightly to mix. Transfer to a serving plate. Heat the oil in a skillet and fry the haloumi over a medium to high heat for 1–2 minutes on each side until golden brown. Arrange the haloumi on top of the salad and serve immediately.

For lemon-dressed haloumi & grape salad, mix 3 tablespoons olive oil with 2 tablespoons lemon juice and 1 teaspoon honey, then season well. Mix ½ cup green and black seedless grapes, halved, with 2½ cups mixed salad leaves and 2 tablespoons fresh cilantro. Chill the leaves and dressing separately. When ready to serve, fry the haloumi as above, toss the dressing with the salad, spoon onto plates, and top with the cheese.

picnic pie

Preparation time **35 minutes**
Cooking time **1½ hours**
Serves **6–8**

¾ cup **lard**
¾ cup **milk** and **water** mixed
2 teaspoons **English mustard**
3 cups **all-purpose flour**
½ teaspoon **salt**

Filling
1 lb lean **pork and leek** or
   Cumberland sausages,
   skinned
1 lb skinless boneless **chicken**
   thighs, chopped
4 oz **bacon**, diced
5 **cloves**, roughly crushed
¼ teaspoon ground **allspice**
small bunch of **sage**
1 **dessert apple**, cored
   and sliced
1 **egg yolk** mixed with
   1 tablespoon **water**
salt and **pepper**

First make the pastry. Heat the lard in the milk and water in a small saucepan until melted then stir in the mustard. Mix the flour and salt in a bowl then stir in the melted lard mixture and mix to a soft ball. Cool for 10 minutes. Mix the sausagemeat, chicken, bacon, cloves, allspice, and plenty of seasoning together in a bowl.

Remove one-third of the pastry and set aside. Press the remaining warm pastry over the base and sides of a deep 7 inch removable-bottomed cake pan. Spoon in half the filling and level. Cover with half the sage leaves, then the apple slices, then spoon over the rest of the filling. Level and top with the remaining sage. Brush the edges of the pastry with the egg glaze.

Roll the reserved pastry to a circle a little larger than the pan, arrange on the pie and press the edges together. Trim off the excess then crimp the edge. Make a slit in the top of the pie, then brush with egg glaze. Cook in a preheated oven, 350°F, for 1½ hours, covering with foil after 40 minutes, when golden. Allow to cool, remove the pan then put the pie, still on the pan base, in the refrigerator for 3–4 hours or overnight. When ready to serve, remove the base and cut the pie into wedges.

For apricot & pickled onion pie, make up the filling as above, but omit the sage and apples, instead adding ⅔ cup sliced ready-to-eat dried apricots and 4–6 drained and sliced pickled onions.

wasabi & ginger tofu salad

Preparation time **15 minutes**
Finishing time **5 minutes**
Serves **4**

4 oz firm **tofu**, sliced into
   thin strips
½ teaspoon **olive oil**

Marinade

1 teaspoon **olive oil**
1 tablespoon **soy sauce**
1 **garlic clove**, crushed
1 inch piece of fresh **ginger
   root**, peeled and finely
   grated
1 teaspoon **lemon juice**
½ teaspoon **wasabi paste**

Alfalfa salad

3 cups shredded **lettuce**
1 small **tomato**, sliced
2 teaspoons finely chopped
   scallion
1 **garlic clove**, crushed
½ **fennel bulb**, finely sliced
1 cup **alfalfa sprouts**
¼ cup **sunflower seeds**
1 tablespoon **lime juice**
½ **avocado**, sliced
salt and **pepper**
1 tablespoon **olive oil**

To make the marinade, mix the olive oil, soy sauce, garlic, ginger, lemon juice, and wasabi in a shallow, nonmetallic dish. Add the tofu, stir well, and chill until required.

To make the salad, put the lettuce, tomato, scallion, garlic, avocado, fennel, and alfalfa sprouts in a bowl. Add the sunflower seeds and lime juice. Season with salt and pepper and toss well. Cover and chill until required.

When ready to serve, heat a heavy skillet and add a small amount of oil. Fry the tofu strips until golden brown on both sides. Peel, pit, and slice the avocado and add to the salad with the oil. Toss and top with tofu. Serve immediately with the alfalfa salad.

For sizzling tofu with gingered greens, arrange 8 oz sliced tofu on a foil-lined broiler rack and brush with a mixture of 2 teaspoons sesame oil and 2 tablespoons soy sauce. Stand 15 minutes, then broil for 4–5 minutes, turning once. Stir-fry 1 lb sliced bok choy with 2 teaspoons sunflower oil, 2 teaspoons sesame oil, 2 chopped garlic cloves, 2 sliced shallots, and 2 tablespoons finely chopped fresh ginger root. Add 1 tablespoon soy sauce, mix well, and serve with the tofu.

salmon & new potato salad

Preparation time **20 minutes**
Cooking time **12–14 minutes**
Finishing time **2 minutes**
Serves **4**

1½ lb baby **new potatoes**,
    thickly sliced
4 **salmon steaks**, about
    4 oz each
6 tablespoons **olive oil**
finely grated zest and juice
    of 1 **lemon**
2 teaspoons **honey**
1 **red onion**, halved and thinly
    sliced
1 tablespoon **capers**, roughly
    chopped, and 2 teaspoons
    brine from the jar
2 oz can **anchovies in oil**,
    drained and roughly
    chopped
small bunch of **parsley**,
    roughly torn
salt and **pepper**

Half-fill the base of a steamer with water, bring to a boil then add the potatoes to the water. Season the salmon and arrange in a single layer in the top of the steamer. Cover and cook the potatoes for 12–14 minutes until just tender, and the salmon for 8–10 minutes until cooked through.

Make the dressing by forking the oil, lemon zest and juice, honey, and seasoning together in the base of a salad bowl. Add the onion, capers, brine, and the anchovies. Drain the potatoes and toss with the dressing while still hot. Skin and flake the salmon, discarding any bones, and arrange on top of the potatoes. Allow to cool, cover, and chill until required.

When ready to serve, tear the parsley over the fish and gently toss the salad together. Serve in shallow bowls.

For new potato salad with horseradish & bresaola, cook the potatoes as above until tender. Make a dressing by mixing ⅔ cup Greek or whole milk yogurt with 1 teaspoon grated horseradish (from a jar) and 4 finely chopped scallions. Add the drained and cooked potatoes and set aside until ready to serve. Stir, spoon onto plates, and top with 4 oz thinly sliced bresaola.

panzanella

Preparation time **15 minutes**
Cooking time **10–15 minutes**
Serves **4**

3 **red bell peppers**, cored,
  seeded, and quartered
12 oz ripe plum **tomatoes**,
  skinned
6 tablespoons **extra virgin
  olive oil**
3 tablespoons **white wine
  vinegar**
2 **garlic** cloves, crushed
4 oz stale **ciabatta bread**,
  broken into small chunks
⅓ cup pitted **black olives**
small handful of **basil** leaves,
  shredded
salt and **pepper**

Place the peppers, skin side up, on a foil-lined broiler rack and broil under a preheated moderate grill for 10–15 minutes or until the skins are blackened.

Meanwhile, quarter the tomatoes and scoop out the pulp, placing it in a sieve over a bowl to catch the juices. Set the tomato quarters aside. Press the pulp with the back of a spoon to extract as much juice as possible. Beat the oil, vinegar, garlic, and salt and pepper into the tomato juice.

When cool enough to handle, peel the skins from the peppers and discard. Roughly slice the peppers and place in a bowl with the tomato quarters, bread, olives, and basil. Add the dressing and toss the ingredients together. Chill until required.

For baked panzanella, halve and seed 2 red bell peppers, leaving the stalks intact. Put into a roasting pan and stuff with 2 skinned and quartered tomatoes, ½ small sliced red onion, 2 chopped garlic cloves, and 4 sliced canned anchovy fillets, if desired. Tear 2 slices ciabatta into coarse crumbs and sprinkle over the top. Sprinkle with black pepper and 3 tablespoons olive oil, then roast at 350°F, for 45 minutes until tender. Sprinkle with a handful of basil leaves and serve hot or cold.

marinated thai beef salad

Preparation time **25 minutes**
Cooking time **15–18 minutes**
Finishing time **5 minutes**
Serves **4**

¾ cup **long-grain white** and
  wild rice, mixed
finely grated zest and juice
  of 2 **limes**
1 lb 6 oz thick cut **sirloin
  steak**
2 tablespoons **sesame oil**
2 **zucchini**
2 **carrots**
4 **scallions**, thinly sliced
2 **garlic cloves**, roughly
  chopped
1 large mild **red chili**, seeded
  and chopped
1½ inch piece of fresh **ginger
  root**, peeled and cut into
  thin strips
2 tablespoons **soy sauce**
4 tablespoons dry **sherry** or
  water
1 tablespoon **Thai fish sauce**
2 teaspoons **superfine sugar**
small bunch of **cilantro** or
  mint, roughly torn

Cook the rice in a saucepan of boiling water for
15–18 minutes or until just tender. Drain, rinse in cold
water, drain thoroughly, and put into a bowl with the
lime zest and juice and toss together. Cover and set
aside. Brush the steaks with the sesame oil then cook
in a preheated skillet over a high heat for 1–3 minutes
each side, depending on preference. Transfer to a
shallow nonmetallic dish.

Cut the zucchini and carrots into long thin slices with a
vegetable peeler, add to the hot skillet with the scallion,
garlic, chili, and ginger and fry briefly for 30 seconds.
Transfer to the dish with the steak. Add the soy sauce,
sherry or water, fish sauce, and sugar to the pan and
warm gently. Pour over the steak and vegetables, allow
to cool, then chill until required.

When ready to serve, transfer the rice to a salad bowl.
Add the vegetables and sauce and the torn herbs and
toss to combine. Cut the steak into thin slices and
arrange on top of the rice salad.

For peppered beef with blue-cheese salad, brush
2 steaks with olive oil then press them onto a mixture
of crushed peppercorns and sea salt flakes to coat.
Pan-fry as above, then wrap in foil and cool. Make a
dressing by mixing ¾ cup plain yogurt with 4 oz mashed
Stilton and 1 finely chopped garlic clove. When ready
to serve, toss 3 cups mixed salad leaves with 1 thinly
sliced red onion and 1½ cups sliced button mushrooms
with the dressing. Spoon onto serving plates. Thinly
slice the beef and arrange on top.

74

mediterranean rice salad

Preparation time **10 minutes**
Cooking time **5 minutes**
Serves **4**

½ cup **broccoli florets**,
  finely chopped
¼ cup finely chopped
  zucchini
½ cup finely chopped mixed
  red and **yellow bell**
  peppers
¼ cup **scallions**, finely
  chopped
½ cup finely sliced
  mushrooms
2 tablespoons **water**
2 tablespoons **pesto**
⅓ cup cooked **brown rice**
⅓ cup cooked **wild rice**
salt and **pepper**

Heat a large skillet or wok, add the vegetables and
the measured water, and cook over a high heat for
3–5 minutes, until the vegetables have softened.
Remove from the heat and allow to cool.

Mix the cooled vegetables with the pesto and cooked
rice, season well, and stir to combine. Cover and chill
until required. Serve topped with a few Parmesan
shavings and some basil leaves, if desired.

For Mediterranean pasta salad, cook the vegetables
as above. Meanwhile, cook 5 oz macaroni in lightly
salted boiling water until just tender. Mix 4 tablespoons
olive oil with 1 tablespoon red wine vinegar, 1 finely
chopped garlic clove, 2 teaspoons sundried tomato
paste, and a small bunch torn basil leaves. Season
well and toss with the pasta and the vegetables.

tandoori chicken salad

Preparation time **15 minutes**, plus marinating
Finishing time **10 minutes**
Serves **4**

¾ cup **plain yogurt**
2 tablespoons **lemon juice**
½ teaspoon ground **turmeric**
1 teaspoon **garam masala**
1 teaspoon **cumin seeds**, roughly crushed
2 tablespoons **tomato paste**
2 **garlic cloves**, finely chopped
¾ inch piece of fresh **ginger root**, finely chopped
3 boneless, skinless **chicken** breasts, thickly sliced
1 tablespoon sunflower **oil**

Salad
4 cups mixed **salad leaves**
small bunch of **cilantro**
4 tablespoons **lemon juice**

Mix the yogurt, lemon juice, spices, tomato paste, garlic, and ginger together in a shallow nonmetallic dish. Add the chicken and toss to coat. Cover and chill for 3–4 hours or until required.

When ready to serve, heat the oil in a large skillet, lift the chicken out of the marinade and add a few pieces at a time to the pan, until all the chicken is in the pan. Cook over a medium heat for 8–10 minutes until the chicken is browned and cooked through.

Meanwhile, toss the salad leaves and cilantro with the lemon juice and divide between serving plates. Spoon the chicken on top and serve immediately.

For tandoori shrimp skewers, thread 13 oz peeled raw jumbo shrimp onto 8 wooden skewers. Place in a large shallow china dish and spoon over the yogurt marinade as above. When ready to serve, lift out of the marinade and cook under a hot broiler for 7–8 minutes, turning until the shrimp are bright pink and cooked through. Serve with salad.

celeriac remoulade

Preparation time **10 minutes**
Cooking time **4 minutes**
Finishing time **5 minutes**
Serves **4**

1 lb **celeriac**, peeled and cut
into matchsticks
12 oz **potatoes**, peeled and
cut into matchsticks
⅔ cup **mayonnaise**
⅔ cup **Greek** or **whole milk
yogurt**
1 teaspoon **Dijon mustard**
6 cocktail **gherkins**, finely
chopped
2 tablespoons **capers**,
chopped
2 tablespoons chopped
tarragon
1 tablespoon **olive oil**, plus
extra for drizzling
1 lb **asparagus**, trimmed
salt and **pepper**

Cook the celeriac in a saucepan of lightly salted boiling water for 2 minutes until softened. Add the potatoes and cook for an additional 2 minutes until just tender. Drain the vegetables and refresh under cold running water. Drain well.

Meanwhile, mix together the mayonnaise, yogurt, mustard, gherkins, capers, and tarragon in a large bowl, season well and set aside. Add the celeriac and potato and stir well to combine. Cover and chill until required.

When ready to serve, heat the oil in a skillet or griddle pan. Add the asparagus and fry for 2–3 minutes until just beginning to brown.

Divide the celeriac and potato remoulade between 4 serving plates. Top with the asparagus spears and serve immediately, drizzled with a little extra olive oil.

For celeriac remoulade with crispy pancetta & eggs, make the remoulade as above then chill. When ready to serve, dry-fry 8 slices of pancetta until crisp. Poach 4 eggs in a saucepan of simmering water until the whites are set and the yolks soft. Lift out of the water with a draining spoon, then serve on a mound of remoulade topped with watercress and the crispy pancetta.

pâté de campagne

Preparation time **30 minutes**, plus chilling
Cooking time **1¾ hours**
Finishing time **5 minutes**
Serves **6–8**

10 oz **bacon**
1 lb 5 oz skinned **turkey leg meat**, taken off bone
7 oz **chicken livers**
1 **onion**, quartered
12 oz **pork belly**, skinned and diced
2–3 **garlic cloves**, finely chopped
small bunch of **thyme**, leaves stripped from stems
6 **cloves**, roughly crushed
6 **juniper** or **allspice berries**, roughly crushed
1½ cups fresh **bread crumbs**
⅓ cup ready-to-eat dried **apricots**, diced
3 tablespoons **port**, **Madeira** or **sherry**
salt and **pepper**

Stretch the slices of bacon until half as long again, using the blade of a large knife. Use the bacon to cover the base and sides of a 2 lb loaf pan so that the slices butt together and hang over the top of the pan. Keep back a few slices for the top.

Mince or finely chop the turkey, chicken livers, and onion in a food processor then mix in a bowl with the belly pork, garlic, thyme, cloves, and juniper or allspice. Stir in the bread crumbs, apricots, and fortified wine. Season well.

Spoon the mixture into the bacon-lined pan and press down well. Cover with the remaining bacon, then fold the overhanging slices over the top. Cover with foil and put the loaf tin in a roasting pan. Pour hot water into the roasting pan to come halfway up the sides of the loaf pan.

Cook the pâté in a preheated oven, 325°F, for 1¾ hours or until the juices run clear when the pâté is pierced with a skewer. Discard the water. Place a small cutting board on top of the pâté and weight down to press it. When cold, chill the pressed pâté overnight.

When ready to serve, loosen the pâté and invert onto a cutting board. Cut into thick slices and serve with radishes, salad, and crusty bread.

For brandied duck pâté with pickled walnuts, omit the turkey and add 1 lb skinned diced duck meat, 3 diced pickled walnuts instead of the apricots, and brandy instead of the fortified wine.

pan bagna

Preparation time **25 minutes**
Cooking time **15 minutes**
Finishing time **2 minutes**
Serves **4–6**

1 **red bell pepper**, cored,
  seeded, and quartered
1 **orange bell pepper**, cored,
  seeded, and quartered
7 oz **eggplant**, thinly sliced
7 oz **zucchini**, thickly sliced
5 tablespoons **olive oil**
3 **garlic cloves**, finely
  chopped
1 round crusty loaf of **bread**,
  8 inches in diameter
2 teaspoons **pesto**
3 oz sliced **pastrami** or **ham**
5 oz **mozzarella cheese**,
  thinly sliced
salt and **pepper**

Arrange the peppers, skin sides up, in the base of a broiler pan then add the eggplant and zucchini in a single layer. Drizzle with 3 tablespoons of the oil, sprinkle with the garlic, and season well. Cook under a preheated broiler for 10 minutes, turning once. Set aside the zucchini and grill the peppers and eggplant for 5 more minutes until softened and the pepper skins charred. Wrap the peppers in foil and allow to cool.

Cut a slice off the top of the loaf then scoop out the center to leave a shell about ¾ inch thick. (Make the soft bread center into bread crumbs, stuffing, or bread pudding.) Mix the remaining oil with the pesto, season, and spoon or brush over the insides of the loaf.

Skin the peppers then arrange the orange peppers in the base of the loaf, cover with pastrami or ham, then the zucchini. Add the mozzarella slices, the red peppers, and finally the eggplant slices along with any of the cooking juices. Replace the lid of the loaf, wrap in waxed paper or foil, and keep in a cool place until required. When ready to serve, cut into thick wedges and serve with salad. Ideal for alfresco dining or a picnic.

For roasted vegetable bread, roast the vegetables as above then layer in the hollowed-out loaf, adding 1½ cups sundried tomatoes, drained of their oil, and 4 canned artichoke hearts, drained and sliced, instead of the pastrami or ham.

pomelo & jumbo shrimp salad

Preparation time **15 minutes**
Cooking time **2 minutes**
Serves **4**

1 large **pomelo**
½ cup **peanuts**, toasted and
  roughly chopped
6 oz raw **jumbo shrimp**,
  peeled
2 tablespoons **grapefruit
  juice**
½ tablespoon **Thai fish sauce**
4 **scallions**, finely shredded
6 **mint** leaves, finely shredded
1 large **red chili**, finely sliced
pinch of **pepper flakes** or
  black pepper
pinch of grated **nutmeg**
4–5 **frisée** or **lollo rosso**
  leaves

Cut the pomelo in half and scoop out the segments and juice. Discard the pith and thick skin surrounding each segment and break the flesh into small pieces. Stir the toasted peanuts into the pomelo flesh and set aside to allow the flavors to blend.

Cook the shrimp in a saucepan of lightly salted boiling water for 1–2 minutes, or until the shrimp turn pink and are cooked through. Remove with a slotted spoon and drain well.

Add the shrimp to the pomelo flesh with the grapefruit juice, fish sauce, shredded scallions, and mint.

Sprinkle the finely sliced chili, pepper flakes or pepper, and nutmeg over the salad and toss together. Line the inside of a bowl with the lettuce leaves and spoon in the salad. Chill until required.

For summer pomelo & avocado salad, cut 1 pomelo into segments as above. Halve 1 galia melon, seed, peel, and cut into cubes. Dice ½ cucumber and 3 tomatoes, discarding the seeds. Toss the pomelo, melon, cucumber, and tomato with 3 tablespoons roughly chopped cilantro and leave for 30 minutes. Just before serving, add 1 peeled, pitted, and diced avocado, if desired, and mix well.

citrus & pomegranate salad

Preparation time **20 minutes**
Serves **4**

4 **oranges**
2 ruby **grapefruit**
3 small heads of green or
    red-tinged **Belgian endive**
1 **pomegranate**
3 tablespoons **olive oil**
1 tablespoon **honey**
2 tablespoons chopped
    cilantro
salt and **pepper**

Cut a slice off the top and bottom of each orange then cut away the pith and skin from the sides with a small serrated knife. Working over a bowl to catch the juices, cut between the membranes to release the flesh and drop the segments into the bowl. Repeat with the grapefruit.

Separate the endive leaves and add to the bowl. Cut the pomegranate in half then pop out the seeds with the point of a small knife, or flex the skin.

To make the dressing, beat the oil, honey, cilantro, and seasoning together then toss with the fruit and endive. Chill until ready to serve.

Stir the fruit salad and spoon into shallow dishes. Serve with warm crusty bread, if desired.

For peppered citrus & strawberry salad, mix the oranges and the grapefruit with 1¼ cups halved strawberries, halved. Toss in the dressing as above, omitting the cilantro and adding ¼ teaspoon roughly crushed peppercorns instead.

tortilla with romesco sauce

Preparation time **25 minutes**
Cooking time **22–24 minutes**
Finishing time **2 minutes**
Serves **4**

2 tablespoons **olive oil**
1¼ lb **potatoes**, thinly sliced
1 **onion**, halved and thinly
   sliced
2 **garlic cloves**, finely
   chopped (optional)
8 **eggs**
2 tablespoons **water**
salt and **pepper**

Romesco sauce
1 **onion**, chopped
1 tablespoon **olive oil**
2 **garlic cloves**, finely
   chopped
4 **tomatoes**, skinned and
   diced
½ teaspoon **smoked paprika**
⅓ cup blanched **almonds**,
   toasted and finely chopped

Heat the oil in a large nonstick skillet, add the potatoes, onion, and garlic, if using, cover, and fry gently for 15 minutes, stirring from time to time until the potatoes are tender.

Meanwhile, make the sauce. Fry the onion in the oil in a saucepan for 5 minutes until just beginning to brown. Add the garlic, tomatoes, and paprika and cook for 2 minutes. Stir in the almonds, season, and simmer for 10 minutes until thick.

Beat the eggs, measured water, and some seasoning together. Pour into the skillet with the potatoes and cook for 4–5 minutes without stirring, until the base is golden and the top almost set. Transfer the pan to a hot broiler and cook the top of the tortilla for 4–5 minutes until browned and set. Loosen the edges of the tortilla and turn out onto a plate. Leave in a cool place until required.

When ready to serve, cut the tortilla into wedges and arrange on small serving plates with spoonfuls of the sauce and a few olives, if desired.

For zucchini frittata with romesco sauce, heat the oil in the skillet then add 1 thinly sliced red onion and 1 lb diced zucchini. Fry gently for 5 minutes until just tender. Beat the 8 eggs with 2 tablespoons water, 3 tablespoons chopped mint and season well. Add to the pan and finish as above. Serve warm or cold with the romesco sauce flavored with 2 tablespoons chopped mint.

sweet potato & haloumi salad

Preparation time **10 minutes**
Cooking time **2 minutes**
Finishing time **10 minutes**
Serves **4**

1 lb **sweet potatoes**, sliced
3 tablespoons **olive oil**
8 oz **haloumi cheese**,
  thinly sliced
2 cups **arugula** leaves

Dressing
5 tablespoons **olive oil**
3 tablespoons **honey**
2 tablespoons **lemon** or
  lime juice
1½ teaspoons **black onion**
  seeds
1 **red chili**, seeded and
  finely sliced
2 teaspoons chopped **lemon**
  thyme
salt and **pepper**

Mix together all the ingredients for the dressing in a small bowl. Set aside until required.

Cook the sweet potatoes in a saucepan of lightly salted boiling water for 2 minutes. Drain well and chill until required.

When ready to serve, heat the oil in a large skillet, add the sweet potatoes, and fry for about 10 minutes, turning once, until golden.

Meanwhile, place the haloumi slices on a lightly oiled foil-lined broiler rack. Cook under a preheated moderate broiler for about 3 minutes until golden.

Divide the sweet potatoes, cheese, and arugula between 4 serving plates and spoon over the dressing. Serve immediately.

tabbouleh with fruit & nuts

Preparation time **15 minutes**,
plus soaking
Serves **4**

¾ cup **bulghur wheat**
¾ cup unsalted, shelled
  pistachio nuts
1 small **red onion**, finely
  chopped
3 **garlic cloves**, crushed
½ cup **flat-leaf parsley**,
  chopped
3 tablespoons **mint**, chopped
finely grated zest and juice of
  1 lemon
1 cup ready-to-eat **prunes**,
  sliced
4 tablespoons **olive oil**
salt and **pepper**

Place the bulghur wheat in a bowl, cover with plenty of
boiling water, and leave to soak for 15 minutes.

Mix the nuts with the onion, garlic, parsley, mint, lemon
zest and juice, and prunes in a large bowl.

Drain the bulghur wheat thoroughly in a sieve, pressing
out as much moisture as possible with the back of a
spoon. Add to the other ingredients with the oil and
season to taste with salt and pepper. Toss the
ingredients to mix well, then chill until required.

For couscous tabbouleh with harissa, soak 1 cup
couscous, ⅓ cup raisins, and ⅓ cup chopped pitted
dates in 1¼ cups boiling water for 5 minutes. Mix
3 tablespoons olive oil with 1 teaspoon harissa
paste, and stir into the couscous with 1 chopped
red onion, a handful of chopped cilantro, and
2 chopped tomatoes.

leeks milanese

Preparation time **25 minutes**
Cooking time **10 minutes**
Finishing time **2 minutes**
Serves **4**

6 tablespoons **olive oil**
4 oz **ciabatta** or rustic **white bread**, torn into pieces
1 **garlic clove**, finely chopped
12 baby **leeks**
2 **eggs**, hard-cooked and roughly chopped
1 tablespoon **red wine vinegar**
1 teaspoon **Dijon mustard**
1 tablespoon **capers**
3 tablespoons roughly chopped **flat-leaf parsley**
salt and **pepper**

Heat 2 tablespoons of the oil in a skillet, add the bread and garlic and fry until crisp and golden. Transfer to a plate and allow to cool. Cover and set aside.

Cut the leeks into 2 or 3 slices, depending on their length, then steam them over a pan of boiling water for 3–4 minutes until just tender. Arrange the leeks in a salad bowl and sprinkle the chopped eggs over the top.

Beat the remaining oil with the vinegar, mustard, and seasoning. Drizzle over the leeks and add the capers and parsley. Cover and chill until required.

When ready to serve, toss the salad gently and sprinkle with the croutons. Spoon onto serving plates and serve immediately.

For milanese pasta salad, cook 10 oz of pasta shells in boiling water until just tender, adding 5 oz of broccoli florets for the last 3 minutes. Drain the pasta and toss with the dressing, eggs, capers, and parsley, as above. Sprinkle with the croutons and serve immediately with a little grated Parmesan.

asian tuna salad

Preparation time **15 minutes**
Finishing time **2 minutes**
Serves **4**

12 oz **tuna steak**, cut into
  strips
3 tablespoons **soy sauce**
1 teaspoon **wasabi paste**
1 tablespoon **sake** or **dry
  white wine**
4 cups mixed **salad leaves**
5 oz baby **yellow tomatoes**,
  halved
1 **cucumber**, sliced into wide
  fine strips

Dressing
2 tablespoons **soy sauce**
1 tablespoon **lime juice**
1 teaspoon **brown sugar**
2 teaspoons **sesame oil**

Combine the tuna strips with the soy sauce, wasabi, and sake. Cover and chill until required.

Arrange the salad leaves, tomatoes, and cucumber on a large serving plate. Cover and chill until required. Mix the dressing ingredients in a bowl and set aside.

When ready to serve, heat a nonstick pan over a high heat and fry the tuna strips for about 10 seconds on each side, or until seared. Arrange the tuna on top of the salad, drizzle with the dressing, and serve immediately.

For asian pork salad, thinly slice 12 oz pork tenderloin instead of the tuna. Marinate in the soy mixture as above and make the salad. Fry the pork in a heated ridged skillet for 5–6 minutes, turning once or twice until cooked through. Serve on the salad drizzled with the dressing.

everyday suppers

pork goujons with fries

Preparation time **25 minutes**
Cooking time **10 minutes**
Finishing time **8 minutes**
Serves **4**

1 lb **pork scallops** or trimmed
  loin steaks
3 tablespoons **all-purpose**
  flour
1 teaspoon **paprika**
small bunch of **thyme**, leaves
  stripped from stems
2 cups fresh **bread crumbs**
finely grated zest of 1 **lemon**
2 **eggs**
1 **onion**, chopped
1 tablespoon **sunflower oil**,
  plus extra for pan-frying
2 **garlic cloves**, finely
  chopped
13 oz can chopped **tomatoes**
salt and **pepper**

Place the pork between two sheets of plastic wrap and beat with a rolling pin until half the original thickness. Cut the pork into thick strips.

Mix the flour, paprika, three-quarters of the thyme leaves, and a little seasoning on a plate. Put the bread crumbs and lemon zest on a second plate and beat the eggs in a large shallow dish. Coat the pork strips one at a time in the flour, then the egg, and then roll in the bread crumbs. Put in a single layer on a baking sheet, cover, and chill until required.

Fry the onion in the oil for 5 minutes until just beginning to brown, stir in the garlic then the tomatoes, a little thyme, and some seasoning. Simmer for 5 minutes until thickened and set aside.

When ready to serve, heat a thin layer of oil in a skillet, add the pork strips, and fry in batches for 2 minutes each side or until golden brown and cooked through. Warm the sauce through then arrange the pork on serving plates with spoonfuls of sauce, lemon wedges, and chunky fries.

For cheesy chicken goujons, use the same weight of boneless, skinless chicken breasts and prepare in the same way as the pork. Omit the thyme and lemon zest, instead mixing ¼ cup finely grated Parmesan with the bread crumbs.

piccadillo tortillas

Preparation time **25 minutes**
Cooking time **about 1 hour**
Finishing time **15 minutes**
Serves **4**

8 oz ground **pork**
8 oz ground **beef**
1 **onion**, chopped
2 **garlic cloves**, finely
   chopped
1 teaspoon **smoked paprika**
1 teaspoon ground **cumin**
½ teaspoon ground **cinnamon**
2 tablespoons slivered
   almonds
2 tablespoons **red wine**
   vinegar
⅓ cup **raisins**
13 oz can chopped **tomatoes**
1¼ cups **chicken stock**

Salsa

1 **red bell pepper**, cored,
   seeded, and chopped
½ **red onion**, finely chopped
small bunch of **cilantro**, finely
   chopped

8 large soft **flour tortillas**
¾ cup **sour cream**
salt and **pepper**

Dry-fry the ground pork and beef in a flameproof
casserole dish with the onion for 5 minutes, stirring
until the meat is evenly browned.

Stir in the garlic, paprika, cumin, and cinnamon then mix
in the almonds, vinegar, raisins, and tomatoes. Add the
stock and some seasoning and bring to a boil, stirring
occasionally. Cover and cook in a preheated oven,
350°F, for 1 hour. Allow to cool, then chill until required.

To make the salsa, mix together the red pepper, red
onion, and cilantro in a bowl and chill until required.

When ready to serve, reheat the piccadillo on the
stovetop for 15 minutes, stirring until piping hot.
Warm the tortillas according to the instructions on the
package. Divide the piccadillo between the tortillas,
and top with spoonfuls of sour cream and salsa. Roll
up and serve immediately.

For chilied tortillas, use 1 lb ground beef instead of
a mixture of pork and beef. Add 1 large dried red chili,
broken in two, and a 13 oz can of red kidney beans
instead of the almonds and raisins. Cook and serve
as above.

spinach & feta phyllo pie

Preparation time **20 minutes**
Cooking time about **1 hour**
Serves **6**

1½ lb fresh **spinach** leaves,
  rinsed
8 oz **feta cheese**, roughly
  crumbled
½ teaspoon **dried red pepper**
  flakes
¾ cup finely grated **Parmesan**
  cheese
⅓ cup **pine nuts**, toasted
1 cup **dill weed**, chopped
¼ cup **tarragon**, chopped
3 **eggs**, beaten
pinch of grated **nutmeg**
8 oz **phyllo pastry**
5–8 tablespoons **olive oil**
1 tablespoon **sesame seeds**
salt and **pepper**

Cook the spinach in a large saucepan, with just the
water left on the leaves after rinsing, over a low heat
until wilted and soft. Drain well pressing out the juices.

Mix the feta into the spinach with the pepper flakes,
Parmesan, pine nuts, and herbs. Mix in the beaten
eggs with plenty of salt, pepper, and grated nutmeg.

Unwrap the phyllo pastry and, working quickly, brush
the top sheet of pastry with a little olive oil. Lay in the
bottom of a lightly greased 8 inch removable-bottomed
cake pan with the edges overlapping the rim of the pan.
Brush the next sheet of pastry and lay it in the opposite
direction to cover the base of the pan. Repeat with
4–6 sheets of pastry, saving 3 sheets to make a lid.

Spoon the spinach mixture into the phyllo pastry shell,
pushing it in with the back of the spoon and to level.

Cut the remaining pastry into 2 inch wide strips. One
by one, brush them with oil and place them on top of
the spinach in a casual folded arrangement. Fold the
overhanging phyllo toward the middle of the pie, sprinkle
with sesame seeds, and bake in a preheated oven,
375°F, for 50–60 minutes. Allow to cool. When ready
to serve, remove from the pan and serve with salad.

For eggplant & almond phyllo pie, fill the pie with
3 sliced and fried eggplants layered with 12 oz sliced
tomatoes, sprinkled with 3 chopped garlic cloves,
4 tablespoons ground almonds, a little ground
allspice, and salt and pepper. Cook as above,
covering with foil if the pie becomes too brown.

bacon & oat-topped mackerel

Preparation time **15 minutes**
Finishing time **10 minutes**
Serves **4**

4 **mackerel**, heads removed,
  boned
4 teaspoons finely chopped
  rosemary leaves
2 slices **Canadian bacon**,
  finely diced
6 tablespoons **rolled oats**
⅓ cup **walnuts**, roughly
  chopped
finely grated zest and juice
  of **1 lemon**
2 tablespoons **olive oil**
2 teaspoons hot **horseradish**
6 tablespoons **Greek** or
  whole milk yogurt
salt and **pepper**

Arrange the mackerel fillets skin side down on a
baking sheet lined with oiled parchment paper or foil.

Mix the rosemary, bacon, oats, walnuts, and lemon
zest together, season then spoon on top of the fish.
Drizzle with the lemon juice and oil. Cover and chill
until required.

Mix the horseradish and yogurt in a small bowl with
a little seasoning, cover, and chill until required.

When ready to serve, remove the cover and bake the
mackerel in a preheated oven, 425°F, for 10 minutes
until the topping is crisp and golden and the fish flakes
easily when pressed with a knife. Serve with salad and
the horseradish sauce.

For baked mackerel with a herb crust, tear 2 oz
ciabatta or other rustic bread into small pieces and
toss with 3 tablespoons chopped chives. Season
and mix with the grated zest and juice of 1 lemon
and 2 tablespoons olive oil. Spoon over the mackerel
and bake as above. Serve with ⅔ cup plain yogurt
mixed with 2 teaspoons wholegrain mustard and
1 teaspoon honey.

pork skewers with parsnip mash

Preparation time **20 minutes**
Cooking time **15 minutes**
Finishing time **10 minutes**
Serves **4**

1½ lb **parsnips**, cut into
chunks
2 sharp **dessert apples**,
such as Granny Smith or
Braeburn, peeled, cored,
and chopped
3 tablespoons **butter**
2 tablespoons **olive oil**
2 tablespoons **red wine
vinegar**
1 tablespoon **honey**
2 teaspoons **fennel seeds**,
roughly crushed
1¼ lb **pork tenderloin**, cubed
16 fresh **bay** leaves (optional)
salt and **pepper**

Cook the parsnips in a saucepan of boiling water for
10 minutes. Add the apples and cook for 5 more
minutes or until the apples and parsnips are tender.
Drain and mash the parsnips and apples with the
butter and a little seasoning. Allow to cool, spoon into
a microwave-proof serving dish, cover with plastic wrap,
and chill until required.

Meanwhile, make the marinade by mixing the oil,
vinegar, honey, and fennel seeds with a little seasoning
in a shallow nonmetallic dish. Add the pork and toss
together. Cover and chill until required.

When ready to serve, thread the pork cubes and bay
leaves, if using, onto 8 skewers. Arrange in a broiler
pan and cook under a preheated medium broiler for
10 minutes, turning once or twice and spooning the
marinade over until the pork is caramelized and
cooked through.

Reheat the mash by piercing the plastic wrap and
cooking in a microwave on full power for 3–4 minutes
until piping hot. Alternatively, return to a small saucepan
and heat gently, stirring constantly, until hot. Spoon
onto plates, top with the skewers, and drizzle the pan
juices over the top. Serve with steamed green beans,
if desired.

For chicken skewers with sweet potato mash,
omit the fennel seeds from the marinade and add
1 teaspoon Cajun spices. Add 1¼ lb boneless
skinless chicken breasts cut into cubes. When ready
to serve, thread the chicken cubes onto 8 skewers
and broil as above. Serve with 1¾ lb sweet potatoes
that have been cooked and mashed.

green chicken kebabs

Preparation time **15 minutes**
Finishing time **10–12 minutes**
Serves **4**

6 tablespoons **plain yogurt**
2 **garlic cloves**, crushed
2 teaspoons finely grated
  fresh **ginger root**
2 teaspoons ground **cumin**
1 teaspoon ground **coriander**
1 **green chili**, seeded and
  finely chopped
large handful of chopped
  cilantro
small handful of chopped **mint**
4 tablespoons **lime juice**
4 skinless, boneless **chicken**
  breasts, cubed
salt

Place the yogurt, garlic, ginger, cumin, ground coriander, chili, chopped herbs, and lime juice in a blender or food processor and blend until fairly smooth. Season lightly.

Place the chicken in a large mixing bowl, pour over the spice mixture and toss to coat evenly. Cover and chill until required.

When ready to cook, thread the chicken pieces onto 8 bamboo skewers. Cook under a preheated medium-hot broiler for 8–10 minutes, turning frequently, until cooked through and lightly browned. Serve immediately with a cucumber salad, with lime wedges for squeezing.

For green cod steaks, mix all the ingredients above together except the chicken and the yogurt. Use the mixture to coat four 6 oz cod steaks. Drizzle with 2 tablespoons olive oil and chill until required. Bake in a preheated oven, 375°F, for 15–18 minutes or until the fish flakes when pressed with a knife.

lamb ragu with toasted walnuts

Preparation time **15 minutes**
Cooking time **1 hour
35 minutes**
Finishing time **10 minutes**
Serves **4**

1 tablespoon **olive oil**
1 lb diced **lamb**
1 **onion**, chopped
2 **garlic cloves**, finely
chopped
½ cup **walnut** pieces, plus
extra to garnish
1 tablespoon **all-purpose
flour**
1¾ cups **lamb stock**
¾ cup **red wine**
2 tablespoons **tomato paste**
1 **bouquet garni**
8 oz **rigatoni** or **penne**
handful of chopped **flat-leaf
parsley**
salt and **pepper**

Heat the oil in a flameproof casserole, add the lamb a few pieces at a time, then add the onion. Fry for about 5 minutes, stirring until browned all over.

Add the garlic and walnuts and fry for a couple of minutes more until the nuts are lightly toasted. Stir in the flour then add the stock, wine, tomato paste, bouquet garni, and a little seasoning. Bring to a boil, stirring occasionally. Cover and cook in a preheated oven, 325°F, for 1½ hours or until the lamb is tender. Allow to cool then chill until required.

When ready to serve, cook the pasta in a large saucepan of boiling water for 8–10 minutes until just tender. Reheat the lamb on the hob, stirring until piping hot. Drain the pasta then toss with the lamb and sprinkle with chopped parsley and a few extra walnuts. Spoon into shallow bowls. Serve with a salad of arugula, watercress, and spinach dressed with lemon juice and sprinkled with Parmesan shavings.

For lamb daube, use 3 oz diced bacon or pancetta instead of the walnuts. Add ⅓ cup pitted prunes with the bouquet garni. Cook as above. Serve with mashed potatoes.

souvlaki burgers

Preparation time **25 minutes**
Finishing time **10 minutes**
Serves **4**

1 lb lean ground **lamb**
small bunch of **cilantro**,
   roughly chopped
1 **red onion**, halved and
   thinly sliced
1 tablespoon **coriander
   seeds**
1 teaspoon **cumin seeds**
1 **garlic clove**
small bunch of **mint**
6 tablespoons **Greek** or
   whole milk yogurt
4 soft floury **burger buns**
2 **small crisphead lettuces**
salt and **pepper**

Put the lamb, chopped cilantro, and half the onion into a food processor bowl. Tip the seeds into a mortar and pestle and grind roughly. Add all but 1 teaspoon to the meat mixture, season, then blitz together. Alternatively, finely chop half the onion and cilantro then mix into the meat with the spices.

Shape the lamb mixture into 4 thick burgers, arrange on a baking sheet, cover, and chill until required. Wrap the remaining sliced onions and chill until required.

Crush the garlic and mint together in a mortar and pestle, add the remaining crushed seeds, the yogurt, and some pepper. Spoon into a small dish, cover, and chill until required.

When ready to serve, broil or barbecue the burgers for about 10 minutes, turning once or twice until browned and cooked right through. Slit and toast the cut sides of the rolls then add the lettuce, burgers, spoonfuls of the yogurt mix, and the remaining onions. Serve with chunky fries, if desired.

For Greek lamb souvlaki, put the ground lamb, cilantro, and red onion in a food processor as above then add 1 large mild, seeded and finely chopped red chili. Divide the mixture into 8, shape into sausage shapes around 8 metal skewers, and chill until required. Broil the koftas for 10 minutes until browned and cooked through. Serve in 4 warmed pita breads, with salad and tzatziki made with 6 tablespoons Greek or whole milk yogurt mixed with ½ diced cucumber and 2 tablespoons chopped cilantro.

chicken & chorizo pappadelle

Preparation time **15 minutes**
Cooking time **35 minutes**
Finishing time **10 minutes**
Serves **4**

2 tablespoons **olive oil**
6 skinless, boneless **chicken**
thighs, cut into chunks
1 **onion**, chopped
4 oz **chorizo**, skinned and
diced
2 **garlic cloves**, finely
chopped
13 oz can chopped **tomatoes**
¾ cup **chicken stock**
1 tablespoon **capers**
12 oz **pappadelle** or
tagliatelle
⅓ cup pitted mixed **olives**
small bunch of **basil**, torn
salt and **pepper**

Heat the oil in a saucepan, add the diced chicken and onion and fry for 5 minutes, stirring until golden. Add the chorizo and garlic and cook for 2 minutes.

Mix in the tomatoes, stock, capers, and seasoning, bring to a boil then cover and cook gently for 30 minutes, stirring from time to time, until the sauce has thickened slightly and the chicken is cooked through. Allow to cool then chill until required.

When ready to serve, cook the pasta in a large saucepan of boiling water for 7–9 minutes until just tender. Meanwhile, add the olives and half the basil to the chicken and reheat thoroughly until piping hot. Drain the pasta, toss with the chicken mixture then spoon into dishes and garnish with the remaining basil leaves.

For chicken & sausage pasta, omit the chorizo, capers, and olives and add instead 3 sliced cooked sausages. Toss with 12 oz cooked pasta shells and some chopped sage leaves.

beet chili & papaya salsa

Preparation time **15 minutes**
Cooking time **1 hour**
  35 minutes
Finishing time **10 minutes**
Serves **4**

1 tablespoon **sunflower oil**
1 **onion**, chopped
2 **garlic cloves**, finely chopped
1 lb raw **beets**, peeled and
  cubed
13 oz can red **kidney beans**,
  drained
1–2 teaspoons **dried red**
  pepper flakes, to taste
2 teaspoons **paprika**
1 teaspoon ground **cinnamon**
13 oz can chopped **tomatoes**
1¾ cups **vegetable stock**
2 tablespoons **red wine**
  vinegar
1 tablespoon **brown sugar**
1 **papaya**, peeled, seeded,
  and diced
½ small **red onion**, finely
  chopped
1 **tomato**, seeded and diced
small bunch of **cilantro**,
  roughly chopped
salt and **pepper**
sour cream

Heat the oil in a flameproof casserole, add the onion, and fry for 5 minutes until lightly browned. Mix in the garlic, beets, kidney beans, pepper flakes, and spices, then add the tomatoes, stock, vinegar, sugar, and plenty of seasoning.

Bring to a boil then cover and cook in a preheated oven, 350°F, for 1½ hours or until the beet is tender. Allow to cool then chill until required.

To make the salsa, mix together the papaya, red onion, tomato, and cilantro and spoon into a serving dish. Cover and chill until required.

When ready to serve, reheat the chili on the stovetop, topping up with extra stock if needed, and stirring frequently until piping hot. Spoon into bowls and top with spoonfuls of the salsa, and some sour cream. Serve with brown rice or warmed tortillas.

For beet, chili, & orange salad, stir the grated zest and juice of 1 orange into the cooked and cooled beet mixture. Spoon onto lettuce leaves and top with low-fat plain yogurt sprinkled with mint leaves and extra orange segments.

feta-stuffed peppers

Preparation time **20 minutes**
Cooking time **10 minutes**
Finishing time **30 minutes**
Serves **4**

¾ cup **bulghur wheat**
3¼ cups **vegetable stock**
2 **orange bell peppers**
2 **yellow bell peppers**
¼ cup **golden raisins**
¼ teaspoon ground **allspice**
4 oz **feta cheese**, crumbled
small bunch of **basil**, torn
1 **onion**, chopped
3 tablespoons **olive oil**
3 **garlic cloves**, finely
  chopped
1 lb **tomatoes**, roughly
  chopped
salt and **pepper**

Cook the bulghur wheat in 2½ cups of the stock in a covered saucepan for 10 minutes.

Lay each pepper on a cutting board and make a cut from the base up toward and around the stem, opening out enough to remove the core and seeds but not so much that the pepper splits in two.

Drain off any excess stock from the cooked bulghur, add the golden raisins, allspice, feta, a little of the basil, and some seasoning. Mix together and spoon into the peppers. Transfer to a roasting pan.

Fry the onion in 1 tablespoon of the oil for 5 minutes until lightly browned. Add the garlic, tomatoes, remaining stock, and a little seasoning. Spoon around the peppers, sprinkle with a little more torn basil then allow to cool. Cover and chill until required.

When ready to serve, drizzle the peppers with the remaining oil and cook in a preheated oven, 400°F, for 30 minutes or until the peppers are softened. Spoon into shallow bowls and garnish with the remaining basil.

For bulghur & feta salad, make up the stuffing with the cooked bulghur, golden raisins, allspice, feta, and a small handful of torn basil leaves. Mix 3 tablespoons olive oil, 1 tablespoon red wine vinegar, and 1 finely chopped garlic clove with salt and pepper. Stir into the bulghur mixture with 4 diced tomatoes and 4 chopped scallions. Chill until required.

smoked haddock fishcakes

Preparation time **30 minutes**
Cooking time **15 minutes**
Finishing time **16–20 minutes**
Serves **4**

1¼ lb **potatoes**, cut into
   chunks
1 lb **smoked haddock**
4 **eggs**
2 tablespoons **butter**
2–3 tablespoons **milk**
3 tablespoons chopped
   chives or **parsley**
2 tablespoons **water**
2⅓ cups fresh **bread crumbs**
4 tablespoons **sunflower oil**
salt and **pepper**

Tartare sauce
¾ cup **sour cream**
finely grated zest of **1 lemon**
2 tablespoons chopped
   chives or **parsley**
3 teaspoons **capers**, roughly
   chopped
2 **gherkins**, finely chopped

Half-fill the base of a steamer with water and bring to a boil. Cook the potatoes in the water in the base for 15 minutes or until tender, and the fish in the top for 8–10 minutes until it flakes when pressed with a knife. Hard-cook 2 of the eggs for 8 minutes.

Skin and flake the fish, discarding any bones. Shell and roughly chop the hard-cooked eggs. Drain and mash the potatoes with the butter, milk, and seasoning. Stir the fish, chopped egg, and chopped herbs into the mash. Divide into 8 portions and pat into thick rounds.

Beat the remaining eggs in a shallow dish with the measured water. Put the bread crumbs in a second shallow dish. Coat the fishcakes in egg on both sides, then coat in the bread crumbs. Arrange on a baking sheet, cover, and chill until required.

Mix all the sauce ingredients with a little seasoning. Spoon into a serving dish, cover, and chill until required.

When ready to serve, heat half the oil in a skillet, add 4 fishcakes, cover, and fry over a medium heat for 8–10 minutes, turning once, until golden on both sides and hot through. Keep hot in the oven while cooking the remaining cakes in the remaining oil. Serve with spoonfuls of sauce, lemon wedges, and a green salad.

For salmon & shrimp fishcakes, use 1 lb salmon fillet instead of the smoked haddock, adding 5 oz roughly chopped cooked shrimp in place of the hard-cooked eggs. Continue as above and serve with lemon mayonnaise.

beery beef with cheesy dumplings

Preparation time **25 minutes**
Cooking time **1 hour**
   35 minutes
Finishing time **20 minutes**
Serves **4**

1 tablespoon **sunflower oil**
1 lb 6 oz **stewing beef**, diced
1 **onion**, roughly chopped
1 tablespoon **all-purpose flour**
1 cup **English beer**
3 cups **beef stock**
2 tablespoons **Worcestershire sauce**
1 tablespoon **wholegrain mustard**
2 **carrots**, diced
2 **parsnips**, diced
½ small **rutabaga**, diced

Dumplings
1 cup **self-rising flour**
½ cup **vegetable suet**
¾ cup grated sharp **cheddar cheese**
2 teaspoons **wholegrain mustard**
4–5 tablespoons **water**
salt and **pepper**

Heat the oil in a flameproof casserole and add the beef a few pieces at a time. Cook for a few minutes, then add the onion and fry over a high heat, stirring, until the meat is evenly browned.

Stir in the all-purpose flour, then mix in the beer, 2½ cups of the stock, the Worcestershire sauce, mustard, and vegetables. Season and bring to a boil, stirring occasionally. Cover the dish and cook in a preheated oven, 325°F, for 1½ hours or until the meat and vegetables are tender. Allow to cool then chill until required.

Mix the self-rising flour, suet, two-thirds of the cheese, and a little seasoning in a bowl, cover, and set aside.

When ready to serve, stir the mustard and enough water into the dumpling mix to make a soft smooth dough. Shape into 8 balls with floured hands. Bring the beef casserole back to a boil on the stovetop, adding the remaining stock, if needed. Stir well and add the dumplings, leaving space between them. Cover and simmer for 15 minutes until the dumplings are fluffy.

Sprinkle the dumplings with the remaining cheese then transfer the casserole to a preheated hot broiler to melt and brown the cheese topping. Spoon into shallow bowls and serve immediately.

For lamb stew with rosemary dumplings, swap the beef for lamb, beer for hard cider, beef stock for chicken stock, and Worcestershire sauce and mustard for a few stems of fresh rosemary. For the dumplings, use 2 tablespoons of chopped rosemary leaves instead of the cheese and mustard.

tricolore cauliflower gratin

Preparation time **15 minutes**
Cooking time **12 minutes**
Finishing time **20 minutes**
Serves **4**

3 **tomatoes**, sliced
4 cups fresh **spinach** leaves
pinch of grated **nutmeg**
1 **cauliflower**, cut into florets
3 tablespoons **butter**
6 tablespoons **all-purpose flour**
1¾ cups **lowfat milk**
1½ cups grated sharp **cheddar cheese**
½ slice of **bread**, torn into tiny pieces
2 tablespoons **sunflower seeds**
2 tablespoons **pumpkin seeds**
salt and **pepper**

Arrange the tomatoes in the base of a shallow ovenproof dish. Steam the spinach for 1–2 minutes until just wilted and spoon over the tomatoes. Sprinkle with a little nutmeg and some seasoning.

Steam the cauliflower for 8–10 minutes until just tender. Meanwhile, melt the butter in a separate saucepan and stir in the flour. Gradually beat in the milk and bring to a boil, stirring constantly, until smooth and thick. Stir in two-thirds of the cheese and season well.

Arrange the cauliflower on top of the spinach, then gently mix together. Pour the sauce over the top. Mix the remaining cheese with the torn bread and seeds then sprinkle over the cheese sauce. Allow to cool, cover, and chill until required.

When ready to serve, remove the cover and cook in a preheated oven, 400°F, for 20 minutes until the topping is crisp and golden and the vegetables are piping hot.

For classic cauliflower cheese, make the cheese sauce as above, omitting the nutmeg and stir in 1 teaspoon English mustard. Cut 1 large cauliflower into florets and cook in a saucepan of boiling water for 8–10 minutes or until tender and drain well. Mix the cauliflower with the sauce, tip into a shallow dish, sprinkle with a little extra grated cheese and 2 tablespoons fine bread crumbs, then broil until golden. Serve with halved broiled tomatoes drizzled with balsamic vinegar.

fish pie

Preparation time **30 minutes**
Cooking time **15 minutes**
Finishing time **40–45 minutes**
Serves **4**

12 oz **salmon** fillet
12 oz **cod** loin
2½ cups **lowfat milk**
1 **bay** leaf
1 **leek**, thinly sliced
1¼ lb **potatoes**, thinly sliced
3 tablespoons chopped
  dill weed
¼ cup **butter**
½ cup **all-purpose flour**
1 cup grated sharp **cheddar
  cheese**
salt and **pepper**

Put the salmon and cod into a skillet, pour over enough of the milk to just cover it, then add the bay leaf and a little seasoning. Bring to a boil then cover and simmer for 8 minutes until the fish flakes when pressed with a knife, adding the leeks for the last 2 minutes.

Meanwhile, cook the potatoes in a saucepan of boiling water for 3–4 minutes until just tender. Drain, rinse in cold water, and drain again.

Lift the fish out of the milk and flake the flesh into large pieces, discarding the skin and any bones. Transfer to a 5 cup, 2 inch deep ovenproof dish. Strain the milk into a pitcher containing the remaining milk and discard the bay leaf. Arrange the leeks on top of the fish and sprinkle with the dill.

Heat the butter in a clean pan, stir in the flour then gradually beat in the milk. Bring to a boil, whisking until thickened and smooth. Season and stir in three-quarters of the cheese. Pour half the sauce over the fish. Arrange the potato slices overlapping on top, pour over the remaining sauce, then sprinkle with the remaining cheese. Allow to cool, then chill until required.

When ready to serve, remove the cover and cook the fish pie in a preheated oven, 350°F, for 40–45 minutes until the top is golden brown and the pie is piping hot. Serve with green beans, if desired.

For smoked haddock & bacon pie, poach 1¼ lb smoked haddock in the milk as above. Broil 4 oz Canadian bacon until crispy, then chop it roughly and add to the pie with 3 tablespoons chopped chives. Finish as above.

shrimp & fennel thai curry

Preparation time **15 minutes**
Cooking time **7–8 minutes**
Finishing time **9–10 minutes**
Serves **4**

1 **onion**, quartered
1 inch piece of fresh **ginger
root**, peeled and quartered
2 **garlic cloves**
1 mild red **chili**, halved and
seeded
1 tablespoon **sunflower oil**
1 tablespoon **Thai green
curry paste**
1¾ cups reduced-fat **coconut
milk**
1¼ cups **fish stock**
2 teaspoons **Thai fish sauce**
3 oz fine **rice noodles**
1 **fennel bulb**, roughly
chopped
4 oz **green beans**, thickly
sliced
small bunch of **cilantro**
3 baby **corn ears**, thickly
sliced
10 oz peeled cooked **shrimp**

Blitz the onion, ginger, garlic, and chili in a blender
or food processor to form a rough paste. Alternatively,
chop the ingredients very finely by hand. Heat the
oil in a saucepan, add the onion paste, and fry for
2–3 minutes, stirring, until softened.

Stir in the curry paste and cook briefly, then mix in the
coconut milk, fish stock, and fish sauce. Simmer gently
for 5 minutes. Allow to cool, then chill until required.

Soak the rice noodles in cold water until soft. Chill
until required.

When ready to serve, reheat the coconut broth, add
the fennel and green beans, and simmer for 5 minutes.
Tear half the cilantro into pieces, add to the broth with
the drained noodles, corn ears, and shrimp and simmer
for 4–5 minutes until piping hot. Ladle into bowls and
garnish with the remaining cilantro.

For chicken Thai green curry, chop 8 boneless,
skinless chicken thighs into bite-size pieces. Fry the
chicken with the onion paste, add 2 small sliced
carrots then the coconut broth ingredients and simmer
for 15 minutes until tender. Allow to cool and chill until
required. Reheat the curry and add the corn ears,
noodles, and cilantro as above.

minted pea & sesame falafel

Preparation time **25 minutes**
Finishing time **5 minutes**
Serves **4**

1⅔ cups frozen **peas**, just
  defrosted
2 x 13 oz cans **chickpeas**,
  drained
1 **onion**, peeled and quartered
1½ teaspoons **cumin seeds**,
  roughly crushed
1½ teaspoons **coriander**
  seeds, roughly crushed
1 teaspoon ground **turmeric**
3 tablespoons chopped **mint**
2 tablespoons **sesame seeds**
1 tablespoon **all-purpose**
  flour
3 tablespoons **olive oil**
salt and **pepper**

Radish cacik
¾ cup **low-fat plain yogurt**
1½ cups finely diced **radishes**
2 inch piece of **cucumber**,
  finely diced
2 tablespoons chopped **mint**

Finely chop the peas, chickpeas, and onion together in a blender or food processor. Alternatively, chop them finely with a knife. Mix in the crushed seeds, turmeric, mint, and seasoning.

Spoon 20 mounds of the mixture onto a baking sheet, then roll into ovals with the palms of your hands. Mix the sesame seeds and flour on a plate, then roll the falafel in the mixture and return to the baking sheet. Cover and chill until required.

Mix all the cacik ingredients together, season to taste, and spoon into a serving bowl. Cover and chill until required.

When ready to serve, heat 2 tablespoons of the oil in a large skillet, add the falafel and fry, turning, until golden brown and piping hot, adding the remaining oil if needed. Serve immediately with the cacik, a green salad, and warmed pita breads.

For carrot & cilantro falafel, boil 1⅔ cups roughly chopped carrots until just tender and use instead of the peas. Substitute fresh cilantro for the mint. Use diced cucumber and chopped cilantro in the cacik instead of the radishes and mint.

mixed mushroom straccatto

Preparation time **15 minutes**,
   plus soaking
Cooking time **25–30 minutes**
Finishing time **8–10 minutes**
Serves **4**

⅓ cup dried **porcini** or mixed
   mushrooms
1¼ cups boiling **water**
1 tablespoon **olive oil**
1 **onion**, chopped
2 **garlic cloves**, finely
   chopped
10 oz small **chestnut
   mushrooms**, halved or
   quartered
13 oz can chopped **tomatoes**
½ teaspoon ground **cinnamon**
1 **bay** leaf
8 oz **pasta shells**
basil leaves
Parmesan shavings
salt and **pepper**

Soak the dried mushrooms in the boiling water for
15 minutes. Meanwhile, heat the oil in a saucepan,
add the onion and fry for 5 minutes, stirring until
just beginning to brown. Stir in the garlic and fresh
mushrooms and fry for 2–3 minutes. Add the tomatoes,
cinnamon, bay leaf, and seasoning.

Add the soaked mushrooms and soaking liquid, bring
the mixture to a boil then cover and simmer gently for
20 minutes, stirring from time to time. Allow to cool and
chill until required.

When ready to serve, cook the pasta in a large saucepan
of boiling water for 8–10 minutes until just tender.
Reheat the mushroom mixture, stirring until piping hot.

Drain the pasta, return to the pan, and toss with the
mushroom mixture. Spoon into shallow bowls and top
with basil leaves and Parmesan shavings to serve.

For mushroom straccatto puff pie, spoon the
mushroom mixture into a 5 cup pie dish and brush
the top edge of the dish with water. Cut some narrow
strips from a 7 oz sheet of ready-rolled puff pastry and
press onto the rim of the dish. Brush the strips with
egg, then cover the dish with the remaining pastry and
trim off the excess. Press the pastry edges together,
flute, and crimp. Bake in a preheated oven, 400°F, for
30 minutes until well risen and golden.

leek & chestnut patties

Preparation time **20 minutes**
Cooking time **15 minutes**
Finishing time **10 minutes**
Serves **4**

1¾ lb **rutabaga**, diced
3–4 tablespoons **lowfat milk**
12 oz **leeks**, finely chopped
⅓ cup ready-to-eat pitted
  prunes, finely chopped
⅓ cup roughly chopped **Brazil
  nuts**
7½ oz can whole peeled
  chestnuts, crumbled
2⅓ cups fresh **bread crumbs**
1 **egg**, beaten
2–3 tablespoons **sunflower
  oil**
salt and **pepper**

Cranberry sauce
2 teaspoons **cornstarch**
¾ cup **vegetable stock**
2 tablespoons **cranberry
  sauce**
1 tablespoon **red wine
  vinegar**
1 teaspoon **Dijon mustard**
1 teaspoon **tomato paste**

Cook the rutabaga in a saucepan of boiling water for 15 minutes until tender. Drain and mash the rutabaga with the measured milk and some seasoning. Spoon into a microwave-proof bowl, allow to cool, cover with plastic wrap, and chill until required.

Meanwhile, mix together the leeks, prunes, Brazil nuts, and chestnuts in a large bowl. Mix in the bread crumbs, egg, and seasoning. Shape into 16 patties, arrange on a baking sheet, cover loosely, and chill until required.

To make the sauce, mix the cornstarch with a little water in a small bowl until smooth. Put the vegetable stock, cranberry sauce, vinegar, mustard, and tomato paste in a pitcher. Add the cornstarch mixture, stir well, and chill.

When ready to serve, heat 2 tablespoons of the oil in a skillet, add the patties, and fry over a medium heat for 10 minutes, turning several times until browned and hot through. Add the remaining oil if needed.

Push the patties to one side of the skillet, add the sauce mix, and bring to a boil, stirring until thickened. Meanwhile, reheat the rutabaga in a microwave on full power for 2½–3 minutes until piping hot. Stir, then spoon onto serving plates and top with the patties and sauce.

For turkey, leek, & prune patties, mix 1 chopped leek with ⅓ cup ready-to-eat chopped prunes, 1 lb ground turkey, 1 cup fresh bread crumbs, 1 egg yolk, and seasoning. Shape into 20 small meatballs and chill until required. Fry in oil as above for 15 minutes. Make the sauce as above and serve with mashed potato instead of rutabaga.

sage & tomato pilaff

Preparation time **15 minutes**
Cooking time **40–45 minutes**
Finishing time **20 minutes**
Serves **4**

1 lb plum **tomatoes**
1 **red bell pepper**, cored,
    seeded, and quartered
1 **onion**, roughly chopped
2 tablespoons **olive oil**
small bunch of **sage**
1 cup easy-cook long-grain
    white and **wild rice** mixed
salt and **pepper**

Cut each tomato into 8 and thickly slice the pepper quarters. Place in a roasting pan with the onion, then drizzle with the oil and season well. Tear some of the sage into pieces and sprinkle over the vegetables. Roast in a preheated oven, 400°F, for 40–45 minutes until softened.

Meanwhile, cook the rice in a saucepan of boiling water for 15 minutes until only just cooked. Drain, rinse in cold water, and drain again well. Mix the rice into the cooked tomatoes and peppers, then cover with foil. Allow to cool and chill until required.

When ready to serve, reheat in a preheated oven, 350°F, still covered with foil for 20 minutes until piping hot. Stir well then spoon into bowls and sprinkle with the remaining sage leaves. Serve with warm ciabatta or herb bread.

For pumpkin & blue cheese pilaff, roast 1 lb peeled, seeded, and diced pumpkin (or butternut squash) with 3 halved plum tomatoes and onion as above. Cook the rice for 15 minutes then drain, allow to cool and then chill until required. Reheat as above, then top with 4 oz crumbled St Agur or other blue cheese and serve.

seared cod with olive butter

Preparation time **20 minutes**
Cooking time **10–12 minutes**
Serves **4**

5 oz **sugar snap peas**
1 lb **zucchini**, sliced diagonally
1 tablespoon **olive oil**
finely grated zest and juice
    of 1 **lemon**
4 **cod fillets**, about 4 oz each
⅓ cup pitted mixed **olives**,
    roughly chopped
¼ cup **butter**
small bunch of **basil**,
    roughly torn
salt and **pepper**

Put the sugar snap peas and zucchini on a large piece of oiled foil, sprinkle with the lemon zest and plenty of seasoning then top with the fish. Drizzle with lemon juice and sprinkle with a little extra seasoning. Seal the edges of the foil to make an airtight parcel. Chill until required.

Beat the olives with the butter and half the basil. Season with pepper, then spoon onto a piece of waxed paper. Wrap tightly and roll into a small log shape. Chill until required.

When ready to serve, put the fish parcel in a broiler pan, open the foil and top the fish with 4 slices of olive butter. Cook under a preheated hot broiler for 8–10 minutes until the fish is browned and flakes when pressed with a knife. Lift out the fish and cook the vegetables for a few minutes more, until just tender and lightly browned.

Spoon the vegetables onto serving plates and top with the fish fillets and any pan juices. Top with the remaining butter, cut into thin slices, and garnish with the remaining basil.

For seared salmon with ginger butter, arrange 4 salmon fillets on top of the sugar snap peas and zucchini. Top with ¼ cup butter mixed with 3 tablespoons chopped fresh cilantro, 1 tablespoon finely chopped fresh ginger root, and 1 finely chopped garlic clove. Cook as above.

food for
friends

lamb with pomegranate couscous

Preparation time **40 minutes**, plus chilling
Finishing time **20–35 minutes**
Serves **4**

2½ lb leg of **lamb**
1 large **pomegranate**
2 **garlic cloves**
small bunch of **mint**, torn
6 tablespoons **olive oil**
1 tablespoon **honey**
finely grated zest and juice
   of 1 **lemon**
1 cup **couscous**
⅓ cup **golden raisins**
½ cup pitted **dates**, sliced
½ **red onion**, finely chopped
1¾ cups boiling **water**
½ cup **pistachio nuts**, cut
   into slivers
2 teaspoons **harissa** (optional)
salt and **pepper**

Remove the bone from the lamb, make a horizontal cut through the thickest part of the meat then open out so it is about 1½ inches thick. Place in a shallow nonmetallic dish. Cut the pomegranate in half and scoop out the seeds. Place half the seeds in a mortar and pestle with the garlic then crush roughly. Mix with half the mint, half the oil, the honey, and half the lemon zest and juice. Season and spoon over the lamb. Cover and chill for at least 3 hours.

Put the couscous into a microwave-proof serving bowl, add the dried fruit, onion, remaining lemon zest and juice, then pour over the boiling water. Allow to cool then cover with plastic wrap and chill until required.

When ready to serve, transfer the lamb to a roasting pan with some of the marinade. Roast in a preheated oven, 425°F, for 20–25 minutes for medium rare, or 30–35 minutes for well done. Lift out the lamb, add the remaining marinade to the hot pan and mix with the pan juices. Pour over the lamb, cover tightly with foil, and allow to stand for 10 minutes.

Add the reserved pomegranate seeds and pistachios to the couscous. Mix the remaining oil with the harissa, if using, drizzle over the couscous then replace the plastic wrap and microwave on full power for 1½–2 minutes until piping hot. Sprinkle the remaining mint over the top and fluff up with a fork. Spoon onto serving plates, top with thickly sliced lamb, and drizzle with pan juices.

vegetable moussaka

Preparation time **20 minutes**
Cooking time **15 minutes**
Finishing time **30–35 minutes**
Serves **4**

5 tablespoons **olive oil**
1 **onion**, chopped
2 **garlic cloves**, finely
    chopped
1 lb **zucchini**, cut into chunks
8 oz closed cup **mushrooms**,
    quartered
1 **red bell pepper**, cored,
    seeded, and cut into chunks
1 **orange bell pepper**, cored,
    seeded, and cut into chunks
2 x 13 oz cans chopped
    tomatoes
2–3 **rosemary** stems, leaves
    stripped from stems
1 teaspoon **superfine sugar**
2 **eggplants**, sliced, sprinkled
    with salt for 15 minutes
3 **eggs**
1¼ cups **low-fat plain yogurt**
large pinch of grated **nutmeg**
3 oz **feta cheese**, grated
salt and **pepper**

Heat 1 tablespoon of the oil in a skillet, add the onion
and fry for 5 minutes, stirring until just beginning to
brown. Add the garlic, zucchini, mushrooms, and
peppers and fry for 2–3 minutes.

Stir in the tomatoes, rosemary, sugar, and seasoning,
bring to a boil then cover and simmer for 15 minutes.
Tip into a shallow ovenproof dish, leaving enough
space to add the eggplants and topping.

Rinse and dry the eggplants. Heat 2 tablespoons of
the oil in a clean skillet and fry half the eggplant slices
until softened and golden on both sides. Arrange,
overlapping, on top of the tomato mixture. Repeat with
remaining oil and eggplants. Allow to cool then chill
until required.

Stir the eggs, yogurt, nutmeg, and a little pepper
together in a bowl, cover, and chill until required.

When ready to serve, stir the yogurt mixture once
more then pour over the eggplants. Sprinkle with
the feta and bake in a preheated oven, 350°F, for
30–35 minutes until piping hot. Spoon onto plates
and serve with garlic bread and salad.

For lamb moussaka, dry-fry 1 lb ground lamb with
1 chopped onion. Add 2 chopped garlic cloves then
mix in a 13 oz can tomatoes and 1¼ cups lamb stock.
Flavor with 1 teaspoon ground cinnamon and a large
pinch nutmeg. Cover and simmer for 40 minutes,
stirring occasionally. Tip into a dish and cover with
eggplants and yogurt mixture as above. Top with feta
or the same amount of cheddar cheese.

marinated angler fish kebabs

Preparation time **15 minutes**, plus chilling
Finishing time **10 minutes**
Serves **4**

1 **onion**, grated
2 **bay leaves**
2 large **rosemary** sprigs
2 **garlic cloves**, crushed
grated zest and juice of
  1 **lemon**
2 tablespoons **olive oil**
1¼ lb **angler fish**, cut into
  cubes
salt and **pepper**

Mint raita
1 cup **plain yogurt**
4 tablespoons **mint**, chopped
pinch of **cayenne pepper**

Mix together the onion, herbs, garlic, lemon zest and juice, and olive oil. Season with salt and pepper and pour over the angler fish. Cover and chill for 1 hour or until required.

To make the mint raita, mix together the yogurt, mint, and cayenne pepper. Cover and chill until required.

When ready to serve, remove the angler fish from the marinade and thread onto skewers. Place the fish under a preheated hot broiler and cook for about 10 minutes, turning occasionally, until browned and cooked right through.

Serve the angler fish kebabs with a bulghur wheat salad and the mint raita.

For marinated chicken kebabs, slice 1 lb boneless, skinless chicken breasts then marinate in the mixture above, using a small bunch torn basil leaves instead of the rosemary and bay. Heat a ridged skillet until hot, then add the chicken and fry until browned on both sides and cooked through.

mushrooms with gorgonzola

Preparation time **20 minutes**
Cooking time **10–15 minutes**
Finishing time **15 minutes**
Serves **4**

4 large **flat field mushrooms**
2 tablespoons **olive oil**
2 **red onions**, sliced
1 teaspoon **superfine sugar**
2–3 **thyme** stems, leaves
   stripped from stems
2 tablespoons **balsamic
   vinegar**
4 **tomatoes**, seeded and
   diced
2¼ cups **sundried tomatoes**,
   drained and sliced
4 oz **gorgonzola cheese**,
   diced
¾ cup **sour cream**
2 cups mixed **watercress**,
   baby **spinach,** and **arugula**
   leaves
4 slices of **ciabatta**
salt and **pepper**

Peel the mushrooms, leaving the stalks intact, then place in an ovenproof dish. Heat the oil in a skillet, add the onions and fry for 5 minutes until softened. Stir in the sugar and cook over a medium heat for 5–10 minutes until very soft and lightly caramelized.

Stir in the thyme leaves, balsamic vinegar, fresh and sundried tomatoes, and some seasoning. Divide the mixture between the mushrooms then cover and chill until required.

Put two-thirds of the cheese in a small saucepan, add the sour cream and a little seasoning then cover and chill until required.

When ready to serve, remove the cover and bake the mushrooms in a preheated oven, 400°F, for 15 minutes until piping hot. Warm the cheese and sour cream mixture, stirring until the cheese has melted. Add the salad leaves to the sauce and cook for 30 seconds.

Toast the bread and divide between 4 serving plates. Scoop the wilted leaves out of the sauce and onto the toast, then put the mushrooms on top of the leaves. Sprinkle with the remaining gorgonzola then drizzle the sauce around the edges of the plates.

For mushrooms with goat cheese, halve 2 goat cheeses, about 4 oz each, and place half on top of each tomato-topped mushroom. Season and sprinkle with a little extra thyme. Bake as above and serve on toasted ciabatta on a bed of risotto.

flounder with applewood crust

Preparation time **20 minutes**
Finishing time **12–14 minutes**
Serves **4**

4 x 5 oz **flounder fillets**
¾ cup dry **white bread
crumbs**
3 tablespoons chopped **flat-
leaf parsley**
1 **garlic** clove, crushed
finely grated zest of ½ **lemon**
¼ cup **walnuts**, finely
chopped
1 oz **Applewood** or
Lancashire cheese, finely
grated
2 tablespoons seasoned **flour**
1 **egg**, beaten
2 tablespoons **butter**
1 tablespoon **olive oil**
salt and **pepper**

Place half the bread crumbs in a blender or food
processor with the chopped parsley and garlic and
blend together until the bread crumbs are slightly green.
Mix these bread crumbs into the remaining crumbs,
together with the lemon zest, walnuts, and cheese.
Season with salt and pepper and mix together well.

Sprinkle a little seasoned flour over each flounder
fillet, then dip the flesh side of each fillet into the
beaten egg. Place the fillets, skin side down, on a
baking sheet and sprinkle the bread crumb mixture
over the fish. Melt the butter with the olive oil and
drizzle over the top. Cover and chill until required.

When ready to serve, remove the covering and cook
the fish on the top shelf of a preheated oven, 400°F,
for 12–14 minutes, or until the crust is golden brown
and the fish cooked through. Serve with wedges of
lemon, fresh herbs, matchstick fries, and a green salad.

For mackerel with a chive crust, tear 1 oz ciabatta
bread into small pieces and mix with the grated zest
and juice of ½ lemon, 2 tablespoons chopped chives,
and some salt and pepper. Place 4 mackerel fillets,
skin side down, on a baking sheet lined with nonstick
parchment paper. Press the crumb mixture on top,
drizzle with 1 tablespoon olive oil, and chill until
needed. Bake as above and serve with a mixed
leaf salad.

braised duck with cranberries

Preparation time **20 minutes**
Cooking time **1 hour
  20 minutes**
Finishing time **30 minutes**
Serves **4**

4 **duck legs**, about 7 oz each
1 **red onion**, cut into wedges
2 tablespoons **all-purpose
  flour**
2½ cups **chicken stock**
½ cup fresh or frozen
  cranberries
1 **orange**, halved and sliced
6 **star anise**
2 tablespoons **soy sauce**
2 teaspoons **Thai fish sauce**
  (optional)
1¼ lb **celeriac**, peeled and
  diced
12 oz **potatoes**, cut into
  chunks
2 tablespoons **butter**
2–3 tablespoons **milk**
salt and **pepper**

Heat a large skillet, add the duck legs, and dry-fry until browned on both sides. Lift out and transfer to a shallow casserole dish. Pour off half the duck fat and then add the onion to the pan and fry for 5 minutes until softened.

Stir in the flour then gradually mix in the stock. Add the cranberries, orange slices, and star anise, then the soy sauce and fish sauce, if using, and some pepper. Bring to a boil then pour over the duck. Cover and cook in a preheated oven, 350°F, for 1¼ hours. Allow to cool and chill until required.

Meanwhile, cook the celeriac and potatoes in a saucepan of boiling water for 15 minutes or until tender. Drain and mash with the butter, milk, and a little seasoning. Spoon into a microwave-proof serving dish and cover with plastic wrap. Allow to cool, then chill until required.

When ready to serve, reheat the duck in the covered dish in a preheated oven, 375°F, for 30 minutes, removing the cover after 15 minutes. Reheat the mash in the microwave on full power for 3–3½ minutes. Stir well, then spoon onto 4 serving plates, top with the duck, and spoon the sauce and fruit around.

For gingered duck with orange, omit the cranberries and spices, instead adding 2 tablespoons finely chopped fresh ginger root, and replacing ¾ cup of the stock with dry white wine.

chickpea & potato tagine

Preparation time **15 minutes**
Cooking time **46 minutes**
Finishing time **10 minutes**
Serves **4**

2 tablespoons **sunflower oil**
2 **onions**, roughly chopped
1 teaspoon **smoked paprika**
1 teaspoon ground **turmeric**
2 teaspoons **cumin seeds**,
  roughly crushed
1 lb **potatoes**, scrubbed and
  cubed
13 oz can **chickpeas**, drained
13 oz can **pinto beans**,
  drained
1 pickled **lemon**, drained
  and quartered
2½ cups **vegetable stock**
small bunch of **cilantro**
4 oz **feta cheese**, crumbled
  (optional)
salt and **pepper**

Heat the oil in a saucepan, add the onion, and fry for
5 minutes until lightly browned. Stir in the spices and
cook for 1 minute. Mix in the potatoes and drained
legumes and stir well.

Add the pickled lemons, stock, and seasoning. Bring to
a boil then reduce the heat, cover, and simmer gently
for 40 minutes until the potatoes are tender. Allow to
cool, then chill until required.

When ready to serve, reheat the potato mixture on
the stovetop, stirring occasionally and topping up
with a little water if needed until piping hot. Spoon into
shallow bowls and top with torn cilantro leaves and feta
cheese, if using. Serve with warmed pita or flat Arab
breads, if desired.

For spiced lamb tagine, fry the onion in the oil as
above, adding 1¼ lb diced, boneless lamb. Stir in
the spices then add 12 oz potatoes, cubed, and a
13 oz can of chickpeas. Omit the pinto beans and
pickled lemon, adding a 13 oz can of chopped
tomatoes instead. Cover and simmer gently for
1 hour. Set aside and reheat when required.
Serve the lamb tagine with couscous and top
with torn cilantro leaves.

beef steaks with mozzarella

Preparation time **15 minutes**
Cooking time **20 minutes**
Finishing time **12–17 minutes**
Serves **4**

2 tablespoons **olive oil**
1 **onion**, finely chopped
1 **garlic clove**, crushed
1 **zucchini**, diced
1 **yellow bell pepper**, cored,
   seeded, and diced
1 **eggplant**, diced
6 plum **tomatoes**, skinned
   and diced
10 **basil** leaves, chopped
2 tablespoons vegetable **oil**
4 **beef** steaks
salt and **pepper**
4 thick slices of **mozzarella**
   cheese

Put the olive oil into a shallow pan over a medium heat and sauté the onion and garlic until golden and crispy. Add the zucchini, yellow pepper, and eggplant, and cook for 5–10 minutes until softened. Add the tomatoes to the pan with a little salt and pepper, then add the chopped basil. Allow the mixture to cool, then cover and chill until required.

Heat the vegetable oil in the same pan over a medium heat. Add the steaks and cook for about 2–4 minutes on each side, or according to taste. Season and remove from the pan.

When ready to serve, place the steaks on a baking sheet. Top each one with a quarter of the vegetables and a thick slice of mozzarella. Cook in a preheated oven, 400°F, for 10–15 minutes until piping hot. Serve immediately.

For peppered steaks with Stilton, coat 4 steaks with 1½ teaspoons roughly crushed black peppercorns and chill until required. Fry in oil as above until just cooked, then transfer to a baking sheet. Sprinkle with 6 oz diced Stilton cheese, then flash under a preheated hot broiler until the cheese has just melted. Serve with a watercress salad and fries.

poacher's pie

Preparation time **30 minutes**
Cooking time **1 hour
20 minutes**
Finishing time **45–50 minutes**
Serves **4**

⅓ cup **dried porcini
mushrooms**
⅔ cup boiling **water**
⅓ cup **butter**
1 tablespoon **olive oil**
1 lb 7 oz **venison**, diced
1 **onion**, chopped
2 tablespoons **all-purpose
flour**
¾ cup **red wine**
1¼ cups **lamb stock**
1 tablespoon **tomato paste**
2 tablespoons **red currant
jelly**
1½ lb **potatoes**
2 tablespoons **milk**
2–3 teaspoons hot
horseradish cream
3 tablespoons chopped
chives
salt and **pepper**

Soak the dried porcini in the boiling water in a small bowl for 15 minutes. Meanwhile, heat one-third of the butter and the oil in a flameproof casserole and add the venison, a few pieces at a time. Add the onion and fry over a high heat for 5 minutes, stirring until browned.

Stir in the flour then mix in the wine, stock, mushrooms and soaking liquid, tomato paste, and red currant jelly. Season then bring to a boil and cover the dish. Bake in a preheated oven, 325°F, for 1¼ hours.

To make the topping, cook the potatoes in boiling water for 15 minutes until tender. Drain and mash with half the remaining butter and the milk. Stir in the horseradish, to taste, the chives, and a little seasoning. Spoon the venison mixture into a 6 cup pie dish. Dot the potato over the top then cover and chill until required.

When ready to serve, remove the cover from the pie and dot the potato with the remaining butter. Stand the dish on a baking sheet then cook in a preheated oven, 375°F, for 45–50 minutes until golden brown and piping hot. Serve with green beans.

For venison cobbler, rub 3 tablespoons butter into 2 cups self-rising flour. Add 4 oz diced Stilton and season well. Set aside until required. Mix in 1 beaten egg and 4–5 tablespoons milk to make a soft dough. Roll out thickly, cut into 8 wedges, arrange on top of the venison, and brush with egg. Bake at 400°F, for 40 minutes until well risen and golden and the venison is piping hot.

roasted trout with arugula pesto

Preparation time **30 minutes**
Finishing time **20–25 minutes**
Serves **4**

13 oz can **navy beans**,
  drained
8 oz cherry **tomatoes**, halved
1 **red onion**, chopped
4 fresh **trout**, heads removed
salt and **pepper**

Arugula pesto
1 ¼ cups **arugula**, plus extra
  to garnish
3 tablespoons **pine nuts**
½ cup finely grated **Parmesan
  cheese**
8 tablespoons **olive oil**

Tip the beans into a large roasting pan, add the cherry tomatoes, onion, and some seasoning and mix together. Slash each side of the trout two or three times with a knife. Tuck the bean mixture in between the slits.

To make the pesto, finely chop the arugula leaves and pine nuts and pound in a mortar and pestle. Alternatively, blitz in a blender or food processor. Mix with the Parmesan, oil, and some seasoning. Spoon a little of the pesto into the cuts in the trout and the inside of the fish, then spoon the rest of the mixture into a small bowl. Cover both and chill until required.

When ready to serve, remove the cover and roast the trout in a preheated oven, 375°F, for 20–25 minutes depending on their size. Test by pressing a knife into the center of the trout through the body cavity: if the fish flakes evenly and is an even color it is ready. Transfer to serving plates and serve with spoonfuls of pesto and extra arugula, if desired.

For roasted lamb with arugula and mint pesto, make up the bean salad as above, put into a roasting pan and top with 8 lamb chops. To make the pesto, use ¾ cup arugula leaves and 5 tablespoons mint leaves. Spoon a little of the pesto over the lamb, then chill until required. Cook as above for 25–30 minutes.

baked salmon with pernod

Preparation time **20 minutes**
Finishing time **25 minutes**
Serves **4**

¼ cup **butter**
7 oz **bok choy**
7 oz **fine asparagus**
4 **salmon** fillets, about
  5 oz each
1 ½ inch piece of fresh **ginger
  root**, peeled and finely
  chopped
8 tablespoons **Pernod** or
  Ricard
salt and **pepper**

Butter 4 large pieces of foil. Separate the bok choy leaves and thickly slice the larger ones. Trim the asparagus and cut each stem into 2 or 3 pieces depending on length. Divide the vegetables between the pieces of foil and place a salmon fillet on top of each one.

Divide the remaining butter between the salmon fillets, sprinkle with the ginger and a little seasoning then drizzle with Pernod. Bring the foil up and over the salmon and seal well. Chill the parcels until required.

When ready to serve, cook the parcels on a baking sheet in a preheated oven, 350°F, for 25 minutes. Unwrap one of the parcels and pierce the center of the salmon. If it flakes easily and the flakes are all one color they are ready, if not, cook for a few more minutes and then retest. Transfer the salmon and vegetables to shallow serving bowls and serve with plain boiled rice.

For baked cod with white wine, use 4 sliced tomatoes instead of the bok choy. Add the asparagus then top with 4 cod steaks. Top with butter, adding a small bunch of chopped basil instead of the ginger and dry white wine instead of the Pernod, and bake as above.

parmesan-breaded lamb chops

Preparation time **15 minutes**
Finishing time **20 minutes**
Serves **4**

¾ cup **all-purpose flour**
1 tablespoon **sesame seeds**
2 racks of French-trimmed
    lamb, about 1¼ lb in total
½ cup freshly grated
    Parmesan cheese
1 cup fresh **bread crumbs**
2 **eggs**, beaten
salt and **pepper**

Season the flour with salt and pepper and mix in the sesame seeds. Dip the lamb into the seasoned flour, coating it evenly all over. Mix together the grated Parmesan and bread crumbs and season with salt and pepper.

Dip the lamb first in the beaten egg and then in the Parmesan mixture and coat all over, pressing the crumbs onto the lamb. Chill until required.

When ready to serve, cook the lamb in a preheated oven, 400°F, for 20–25 minutes. Cut the lamb into 4 pairs of chops and serve with lemon halves, new potatoes, carrot matchsticks, beans, and parsley.

For red currant & rosemary lamb chops, mix 3 tablespoons red currant jelly, 4 teaspoons finely chopped rosemary leaves, 2 chopped garlic cloves, and 1 teaspoon roughly crushed black peppercorns. Arrange the racks of lamb with the fat uppermost, and spread with the jelly mix. Chill until needed then roast as above.

bacon & sundried tomato chicken

Preparation time **35 minutes**
Finishing time **30–35 minutes**
Serves **4**

1½ lb **potatoes**, peeled and
thinly sliced
1 **onion**, thinly sliced
2 **garlic cloves**, finely
chopped (optional)
1¼ cups **heavy cream**
2 tablespoons **butter**
4 boneless, skinless **chicken**
breasts, about 5 oz each
1 cup **sundried tomatoes** in
oil, drained
8 large **sage** leaves
8 slices **bacon**
salt and **pepper**

Blanch the potatoes in a saucepan of boiling water for
4–5 minutes until almost cooked. Drain into a colander.
Layer the potatoes in a buttered 5 cup ovenproof dish
with the onions, garlic if using, and seasoning. Pour the
cream over the top and dot with butter. Cover and chill
until required.

Make a slit down the side of each chicken breast and
enlarge the slit to make a pocket. Divide the sundried
tomatoes between the pockets, adding a sage leaf to
each. Press a sage leaf on the top of each breast and
sprinkle with seasoning.

Stretch the slices of bacon by pressing a large cook's
knife along the length of each. Wrap one slice around
each breast, then wrap a second at a different angle to
the first to make a crisscross pattern. Put the breasts
into a roasting pan with the ends of the bacon tucked
underneath. Cover and chill until required.

When ready to serve, remove the covers and bake the
chicken and potatoes in a preheated oven, 400°F, for
30–35 minutes, alternating oven positions once during
cooking until the potatoes and bacon are golden. Test
the chicken by pressing a small knife into the center of
the breast; juices will run clear when ready. Transfer to
serving plates and serve with an arugula salad, if desired.

For pancetta & blue cheese chicken, stuff the
chicken breasts with 4 oz dolcelatte in place of the
sundried tomatoes. Wrap in 8 slices of pancetta
instead of the bacon. Drizzle with 1 tablespoon olive
oil and continue as above.

crab & sweet potato cakes

Preparation time **10 minutes**
Cooking time **10 minutes**
Finishing time **10 minutes**
Serves **4**

1 lb **sweet potatoes**
8 oz **Yukon gold potatoes**
1 small **egg**, beaten
8 oz white **crabmeat**
½ teaspoon **paprika**
3 tablespoons **all-purpose flour**
oil, for pan-frying
salt and **pepper**

Peel both types of potatoes and cook in a saucepan of lightly salted boiling water for about 15 minutes or until soft when pierced with the tip of a knife. Drain well, return to the pan, and roughly mash. Allow to cool.

When the potatoes are cold, add the beaten egg, season with salt and pepper, and mix well. Add the crabmeat and mix into the potato mash with the paprika and flour.

With floured hands, shape 2 tablespoons of the mixture into a flat cake. Repeat until all the mixture has been used, then chill the crab cakes until required.

When ready to serve, heat the oil in a large skillet and fry 4 crab cakes at a time for 3–4 minutes, turning occasionally, until they are golden brown on all sides and heated through. Remove from the oil and drain well. Keep warm while cooking the rest of the crab cakes. Serve immediately with garlic mayonnaise and crisp salad leaves.

For garlic mayonnaise to serve as an accompaniment, place 2 crushed garlic cloves and 1 small red chili, seeded and chopped, in a blender or food processor. Add 1 egg yolk and 1 tablespoon white wine vinegar and process well. With the motor still running, slowly add ⅔ cup olive oil in a thin stream. If this is added slowly enough, the egg mixture will gradually thicken into a mayonnaise.

shallot tart tatin

Preparation time **25 minutes**
Cooking time **12 minutes**
Finishing time **25–30 minutes**
Serves **4**

1 lb **shallots**, peeled
¼ cup **butter**
2 tablespoons **light brown sugar**
3 tablespoons **cider vinegar**
a few **thyme** sprigs
8 oz **puff pastry**, defrosted if frozen
flour, for dusting
salt and **pepper**

Cut any large shallots in half. Melt the butter in an 8 inch skillet. Add the shallots and fry over a medium heat for 5 minutes until just beginning to brown.

Add the sugar and fry for 5 more minutes or until caramelized, turning from time to time so that the shallots cook evenly. Add the vinegar, leaves from the thyme sprigs, and some seasoning and cook for 2 minutes.

If your skillet has a metal handle then leave the shallots to cool for 20 minutes in the pan, if not transfer to a heavy-based 8 inch buttered round cake pan.

Roll out the pastry on a lightly floured surface and trim to an 8 inch circle. Arrange on top of the onions and tuck down the sides of the skillet or cake pan. Cover and chill until required.

When ready to serve, remove the cover and bake in a preheated oven, 400°F, for 25–30 minutes until the pastry is well risen and golden. Allow to stand for 5 minutes, then loosen the edges with a knife. Cover with a serving plate or cutting board and invert the skillet or cake pan onto the plate then remove. Serve warm, cut into wedges, with a green leaf salad.

For shallot, apple, & walnut tart tatin, reduce the shallots to 12 oz and add 1 dessert apple, cored, peeled, and cut into 8 slices. Fry as above, adding 2 tablespoons walnut pieces with the sugar.

tindori & green mango curry

Preparation time **20 minutes**
Cooking time **35 minutes**
Finishing time **5 minutes**
Serves **4**

½ cup **green lentils**, rinsed
3 tablespoons **vegetable oil**
1 teaspoon ground **turmeric**
2 teaspoons **garam masala**
1 teaspoon **cumin seeds**
1 teaspoon **black onion
seeds**
1 **red chili**, finely chopped
1 **green chili**, finely chopped
3 large **tomatoes**, chopped
8 oz **tindori**, rinsed and
trimmed
2 tablespoons **brown sugar**
1 tablespoon **tamarind paste**
⅔ cup boiling **water**
1 small **green mango**
1 small **red onion**, finely
chopped
handful of chopped **cilantro**
salt and **pepper**

Cook the rinsed lentils in a saucepan of boiling water
for 20 minutes until soft. Drain well.

Meanwhile, heat the oil in a large saucepan and fry
the turmeric, garam masala, cumin seeds, and black
onion seeds for 1–2 minutes or until the spices are
sizzling and the mustard seeds begin to pop.

Add the chopped chilies and the tomatoes together
with the drained lentils and tindori. Cover the pan and
simmer gently for 10 minutes, stirring occasionally. Mix
the brown sugar and tamarind paste with the boiling
water and add to the pan. Stir well and simmer for an
additional 5 minutes. Season to taste and allow to cool.
Cover and chill until required.

Shred the mango finely and mix with the red onion
and cilantro. Cover and chill until required.

When ready to serve, reheat the curry gently over
a medium heat until piping hot. Top with the green
mango and red onion mixture and serve with chapatis.

classic paella

Preparation time **40 minutes**
Cooking time 1¼ **hours**
Finishing time **15 minutes**
Serves **6**

4 **garlic cloves**
small bunch of **mixed herbs**
⅔ cup **dry white wine**
8 cups hot **chicken stock**
   or water
2 lb fresh **mussels**, scrubbed
4 small **squid**, cleaned and
   sliced into rings
4 tablespoons **olive oil**
1 large **onion**, finely chopped
1 **red bell pepper**, cored,
   seeded, and chopped
4 large ripe **tomatoes**, skinned,
   seeded, and chopped
12 skinless, boneless **chicken**
   thighs, cut into bite-size
   pieces
2½ cups **paella rice**
large pinch of **saffron** threads,
   crushed
1 cup fresh or frozen **peas**
12 large raw peeled **shrimp**
salt and **pepper**

Slice 2 garlic cloves and crush the rest. Put the slices in a large heavy pan with the herbs, wine, ⅔ cup of the stock or water, and season well. Add the mussels, cover the pan, and bring to a boil. Simmer for 5 minutes until the mussels open. Remove the mussels, discard any which remain closed, and chill the remainder until required. Strain the liquid and reserve.

Fry the squid in half the oil for 5 minutes, stirring frequently. Add the onion, red pepper, and crushed garlic and cook gently, stirring frequently, for 5 minutes until softened. Add the mussel cooking liquid and tomatoes and season. Bring to a boil, then simmer over a gentle heat, stirring, for 15–20 minutes until the mixture is thick. Transfer to a bowl.

Sauté the chicken in the remaining oil for 5 minutes. Add the rice and turn it in the oil for 3 minutes. Stir the squid mixture into the pan. Add about one-third of the remaining stock and saffron and bring to a boil, stirring constantly. Cover and simmer for 30 minutes. Add more stock as the rice becomes dry and stir frequently. When the chicken is cooked, the rice is tender but still firm and almost all the liquid has been absorbed, remove from the heat and allow to cool. Cover and chill until required.

When ready to serve, reheat the paella over a gentle heat. Check the seasoning and add the peas and shrimp, simmer, stirring, for 5 minutes, adding a little more stock or water if required. Add the mussels, cover the pan, and cook for 5 minutes or until the mussels are hot. Serve immediately.

maple lamb with sweet potatoes

Preparation time **20 minutes**
Finishing time **30–45 minutes**
Serves **4**

2 lb **sweet potatoes**, peeled
   and cut into 1 inch cubes
2 **onions**, roughly chopped
3 teaspoons **fennel seeds**
pared rind and juice of 1 large
   orange
4 tablespoons **olive oil**
2 racks of **lamb**, about
   1 lb each
2 tablespoons **maple syrup**
salt and **pepper**

Put the potato cubes and onions into a large roasting pan then sprinkle with the fennel seeds and seasoning. Tuck the orange rind strips in among the potatoes and drizzle with the orange juice and oil.

Make a space in the potatoes for the lamb and put in a single layer with the fat uppermost. Season the fat, cover, and chill until required.

When ready to serve, remove the cover and drizzle the lamb fat with the maple syrup. Roast in a preheated oven, 400°F, for 20–25 minutes for medium rare or 30–35 minutes for well done. Cover with foil toward the end of cooking for well done lamb.

Lift the lamb out of the pan, wrap in foil, and allow to stand for 10 minutes. Stir the potatoes and continue cooking for another 10 minutes until brown around the edges. Spoon onto serving plates, cut between the bones of the lamb, and serve 3–4 chops per portion. Serve with steamed green beans, if desired.

For honeyed lamb with rosemary leeks, drizzle the lamb with 1 tablespoon honey instead of the maple syrup and roast on its own. Slice 1 lb leeks, stir-fry with 2 tablespoons olive oil and a handful of finely chopped rosemary. Stir in 1 cup frozen peas and 3 tablespoons sour cream. Serve the lamb and vegetables with new potatoes.

parmesan soufflés with carrots

Preparation time **25 minutes**
Cooking time **25 minutes**
Finishing time **25–30 minutes**
Serves **4**

5 tablespoons **butter**
¾ cup finely grated **Parmesan cheese**
¾ cup finely grated **cheddar cheese**
¼ cup **all-purpose flour**
1¼ cups **lowfat milk**
1 teaspoon **Dijon mustard**
4 **eggs**, separated, plus
   1 extra **egg white**
salt and **cayenne pepper**

Glazed carrots
2 tablespoons **butter**
12 oz baby **carrots**, halved lengthwise
3 tablespoons **Marsala** or **sherry**
2 tablespoons chopped **chives**

First make the glazed carrots. Melt the butter in a skillet, add the carrots, cover, and fry gently for 15 minutes, shaking the pan from time to time. Add the Marsala or sherry, season well, and cook for 10 minutes until tender. Allow to cool then chill until required.

Meanwhile, butter the insides of 4 soufflé dishes, about 4 inches in diameter and 2½ inches tall. Mix the cheeses together, add 1 tablespoon to each dish then tilt the dishes until the insides are coated with cheese.

Melt the remaining butter in a saucepan, stir in the flour, and cook for 1 minute. Beat in the milk and bring to a boil, beating continuously until very thick and smooth. Take off the heat and mix in the remaining cheese, egg yolks, mustard, salt to taste, and a large pinch of cayenne. Allow to cool for 10 minutes, then gradually beat in the egg yolks. Cool.

Beat the egg whites until stiff, then fold a large spoonful into the cooled cheese sauce. Add the remainder and gently fold in. Divide the mixture between the soufflé dishes then freeze (uncovered) in the coldest part of the freezer until required.

When ready to serve, wrap the dishes with folded nonstick parchment paper that stands 1½ inches above the dishes and tie with string (see page 8). Cook in a preheated oven, 350°F, for 25–30 minutes until golden brown and risen. The edges should be set and the center still soft. Reheat the carrots and sprinkle with the chives. Transfer the soufflé dishes to serving plates and spoon the carrots around them.

kashmiri pumpkin curry

Preparation time **20 minutes**
Cooking time **20 minutes**
Finishing time **5 minutes**
Serves **4**

2 **onions**, quartered
2 **garlic cloves**
1½ inch piece of fresh **ginger root**, peeled and sliced
1 large **red chili**, halved and seeded
1 teaspoon **cumin seeds**, roughly crushed
1 teaspoon **coriander seeds**, roughly crushed
5 **cardamom pods**, crushed
2¾ lb **pumpkin**, seeded and peeled
2 tablespoons **sunflower oil**
1 tablespoon **butter**
1 teaspoon ground **turmeric**
1 teaspoon **paprika**
1 **cinnamon** stick, halved
1¾ cups **vegetable stock**
⅔ cup **heavy cream**
½ cup **pistachio nuts**, roughly chopped
small bunch of **cilantro**, torn
salt and **pepper**

Finely chop the onion, garlic, ginger, and chili in a blender or food processor, or finely chop by hand, and mix with the crushed cumin, coriander, and cardamom.

Slice the pumpkin into 1 inch wedges, then cut the wedges in half. Heat the oil and butter in a large skillet, add the pumpkin pieces and fry for 5 minutes until lightly browned. Push the pumpkin to one side of the pan then add the onion mixture and fry until beginning to brown.

Add the turmeric, paprika, and cinnamon, cook briefly then stir in the stock. Season and bring to a boil. Cover and simmer for 10 minutes until the pumpkin is almost cooked. Allow to cool, cover, and chill until required.

When ready to serve, add half the cream, half the pistachios, and half the cilantro leaves. Reheat until piping hot. Drizzle with the remaining cream, and sprinkle with the remaining pistachios and cilantro. Serve with naan breads and a tomato and onion salad.

For kashmiri chicken curry, cut 8 boneless skinless chicken thighs into large chunks and use instead of the pumpkin. Fry in the oil and butter, then simmer in the stock for 30 minutes. Reheat and finish as above.

balsamic chicken with roots

Preparation time **20 minutes**
Cooking time **4–5 minutes**
Finishing time **40–45 minutes**
Serves **4**

4 **chicken thighs**, skinned
4 **chicken drumsticks**,
  skinned
3 tablespoons **balsamic**
  vinegar
3 tablespoons **white wine**
small bunch fresh **sage**
1 lb 2 oz **potatoes**, scrubbed
  and cut into wedges
9 oz **parsnips**, peeled and
  cut into wedges
9 oz baby **carrots**, scrubbed
  and halved lengthwise
2 small **red onions**, cut into
  wedges
4 tablespoons **olive oil**
salt and **pepper**

Slash each chicken piece 2 or 3 times with a small knife then put into a large plastic bag with the balsamic vinegar, wine, sage, and some seasoning. Seal the bag well and chill for 3–4 hours or until required.

Cook the potatoes in a saucepan of boiling water for 4–5 minutes until almost tender, then drain well and tip into a large roasting pan. Add the parsnips, carrots, and onion wedges, cover, and set aside until required.

When ready to serve, tip the chicken and the marinade into the roasting pan. Drizzle the oil over the vegetables and sprinkle with a little seasoning. Roast in a preheated oven, 400°F, for 40–45 minutes, turning the vegetables once or twice until golden and the juices run clear when the chicken is pierced with a small knife. Serve with a mixed leaf salad.

For balsamic chicken with Mediterranean vegetables, marinate the chicken in the same way, using 3 stems of rosemary instead of the sage. Use 1 lb scrubbed new potatoes (no need to blanch), 1 lb zucchini wedges, 3 quartered and cored red bell peppers and 1 bulb of garlic, separated into cloves but not peeled. Place in a roasting pan, drizzle with oil, and roast with the chicken as above.

game pie

Preparation time **45 minutes**
Cooking time **1½ hours**
Finishing time **25–30 minutes**
Serves **4**

2 tablespoons **butter**
1 tablespoon **olive oil**
1 oven-ready **pheasant**,
   halved
1 oven-ready **pigeon** or
   squab, halved
2 **rabbit** or **chicken** leg joints
1 large **onion**, roughly
   chopped
4 oz **bacon**, diced
2 tablespoons **all-purpose**
   flour
¾ cup **red wine**
1¾ cups **chicken stock**
2 tablespoons **red currant**
   jelly
1 teaspoon **juniper** or **allspice**
   berries, roughly crushed
1 **bouquet garni**
12 oz ready-made **puff pastry**
flour, for dusting
beaten **egg**, for glazing
salt and **pepper**

Heat the butter and oil in a large skillet then fry the game, in batches, until browned. Lift out and put into a large casserole dish. Add the onion and bacon to the skillet and fry for 5 minutes, stirring until golden. Mix in the flour then stir in the wine, stock, and red currant jelly. Add the berries, bouquet garni, and seasoning, then bring to a boil. Tip the sauce over the game, cover, and cook in a preheated oven, 325°F, for 1¼ hours. Allow to cool.

Lift out the game and take the meat off the bone. Return to the sauce, discard the bouquet garni then spoon into a 5 cup pie dish.

Roll the pastry on a lightly floured surface until a little larger than the top of the pie dish. Cut ½ inch wide strips from the edges and stick onto the dish rim with beaten egg. Brush the pastry strips with egg and lay the sheet of pastry on top. Press down, trim off the excess then flute the edges. Cut leaves from reformed trimmings. Chill, uncovered, until required.

When ready to serve, brush the pie with beaten egg then cook in a preheated oven, 400°F, for 25–30 minutes until golden and piping hot inside. Serve with steamed Brussels sprouts and braised red cabbage, if desired.

For beef & mushroom pie, fry 1½ lb diced stewing beef and 5 oz quartered mushrooms in the butter and oil. Mix with the fried onion and bacon, then the flour and stock. Continue as above but cook for 2 hours in the oven before making up the pie as above.

seafood stew with gremolata

Preparation time **20 minutes**
Cooking time **30 minutes**
Finishing time **15 minutes**
Serves **4**

½ teaspoon **saffron** threads
2 tablespoons boiling **water**
3 tablespoons **olive oil**
1 **onion**, roughly chopped
2 **yellow bell peppers**,
   quartered, seeded, and
   thickly sliced
13 oz can chopped **tomatoes**
⅔ cup **fish stock**
¾ cup **dry white wine**
2 tablespoons **sundried**
   tomato paste
13 oz baby new **potatoes**,
   scrubbed
4 tablespoons roughly
   chopped **flat-leaf parsley**
finely grated zest of 1 **lemon**
1–2 **garlic cloves**, finely
   chopped
1¼ lb **cod loin**, cut into
   large cubes
8 oz mixed **shellfish** and
   squid
salt and **pepper**

Put the saffron into a small cup, cover with the boiling water and let soak.

Heat the oil in a flameproof casserole, add the onion and peppers, and fry gently for 5 minutes until just beginning to brown. Stir in the tomatoes, fish stock, and wine. Mix in the tomato paste and some seasoning, then add the potatoes and saffron with its soaking water. Bring to a boil then cover and simmer for 20 minutes until the potatoes are just tender. Allow to cool, cover, and chill until required.

To make the gremolata, mix together the parsley, lemon zest, and garlic, cover, and chill until required.

When ready to serve, reheat the sauce then add the cod and seafood. Cover and simmer gently for 15 minutes until the cod is just tender. Be careful not to overcook or the cod will fall apart. Sprinkle with a little of the gremolata, then ladle into shallow bowls. Serve immediately with warm rustic bread, salad, and the remaining gremolata for sprinkling.

For cod stew with pesto, add 4 teaspoons basil pesto to the sauce instead of the saffron. Use 9 oz cooked peeled shrimp instead of the mixed shellfish, and sprinkle the finished dish with chopped basil leaves instead of gremolata.

desserts

apricot fool with shortbread

Preparation time **30 minutes**
Cooking time **30–35 minutes**
Finishing time **5 minutes**
Serves **4**

10 **cardamom pods**, split
1¼ cups ready-to-eat dried
  apricots
¼ cup **superfine sugar**
1¼ cups **water**
⅔ cup **heavy cream**
5 oz carton ready-made
  custard

Cardamom shortbread
seeds from 10 **cardamom
  pods**, finely crushed
1¼ cups **all-purpose flour**
3 tablespoons **cornstarch**
¼ cup **superfine sugar**, plus
  extra for sprinkling
½ cup **butter**, diced

Put the cardamom pods and seeds into a saucepan with the apricots, sugar, and water. Bring to a boil then cover and simmer for 10 minutes until tender. Remove the cardamom pods, puree the apricot mixture, and allow to cool.

Meanwhile, make the shortbread. Put the crushed cardamom seeds into the bowl of a food processor with the flour, cornstarch, sugar, and butter and blitz until the mixture forms a ball. Alternatively, put the ingredients into a bowl and blend the butter in with your fingertips until the mixture resembles bread crumbs. Squeeze the crumbs together to form a ball.

Tip the mixture into a 9 inch ungreased removable-bottomed tart pan and press into an even layer with your hands. Prick the surface and bake in a preheated oven, 325°F, for 20–25 minutes until pale golden. Mark into thin wedges then sprinkle with a little sugar and allow to cool in the pan.

Whip the cream in a bowl until soft swirls form, then fold in the custard. Add the apricot puree and lightly swirl together until the mixture is marbled. Spoon into 4 glass tumblers. Cover and chill until required.

When ready to serve, put each tumbler onto a saucer and add 2 shortbread fingers.

For summer berry fool with shortbread, mix 2½ cups defrosted and pureed mixed frozen summer fruits into the custard and cream mixture and add 1 teaspoon lavender flowers. Serve with shortbreads made with 1 teaspoon dried lavender flowers instead of the cardamom seeds.

chocolate & gingersnap mousse

Preparation time **25 minutes**,
  plus chilling
Cooking time **10 minutes**
Finishing time **5 minutes**
Serves **4**

1 cup **semisweet chocolate**,
  broken into pieces
3 tablespoons strong **coffee**
3 **eggs**, separated
10 **gingersnap cookies**
3 tablespoons **butter**
4 tablespoons **sour cream**
sifted instant **cocoa**

Melt the chocolate in a bowl set over a saucepan of simmering water. Stir in the coffee, then gradually mix in the egg yolks one at a time. Allow to cool slightly.

Place the cookies in a plastic bag and crush with a rolling pin to make fine crumbs. Melt the butter in a small saucepan then stir in the crumbs. Line 4 ⅔ cup ramekin dishes with plastic wrap so that the wrap overhangs the edges of the dishes. Divide half the crumbs between the bases of the dishes and press flat.

Beat the egg whites until soft peaks, then stir a spoonful into the chocolate mixture to loosen it slightly. Fold in the remaining egg whites using a metal spoon. Pour the mousse mixture into the dishes, level the surfaces then sprinkle with the remaining crumbs. Chill for 4–5 hours or until set.

When ready to serve, lift the puddings out of the dishes using the plastic wrap and then peel the plastic wrap away. Top each pudding with a spoonful of sour cream and then decorate with a light dusting of instant cocoa.

For chocolate & orange mousses, leave out the cookie crumb mixture and flavor the chocolate mousse with 2 tablespoons orange juice and 2 tablespoons Grand Marnier or Cointreau instead of the coffee. Pour into small glasses, then top with sour cream and instant cocoa as above.

plum tarts with saffron custard

Preparation time **30 minutes**
Cooking time **12–15 minutes**
Finishing time **5 minutes**
(optional)
Serves **6**

7 oz ready-rolled **puff pastry**
¼ cup **butter**, at room
temperature
¼ cup **superfine sugar**
½ cup ground **almonds**
1 **egg yolk**
6 ripe **red plums**, about
10 oz, pitted and thickly
sliced
sifted **confectioners' sugar**

Custard
4 **egg yolks**
¼ cup **superfine sugar**, plus
a little extra for sprinkling
1 teaspoon **cornstarch**
large pinch of **saffron** threads
1¼ cups **lowfat milk**

Cut the pastry into 6 even rectangles. Knock up and flute the edges with a sharp knife then transfer to a lightly greased baking sheet. Prick the centers of the pastries.

Cream the butter and sugar together, then mix in the ground almonds and egg yolk. Divide the mixture between the pastry rectangles, then spread into a thin layer, leaving a border of pastry around the edges.

Arrange the plums on top of the almond mixture, then bake in a preheated oven, 400°F, for 12–15 minutes until the pastry is well risen and golden. Loosen the bases of the tarts with a spatula then allow to cool.

To make the custard, beat the egg yolks, sugar, cornstarch, and saffron together in a bowl. Heat the milk in a saucepan until just boiling then gradually beat into the egg yolks. Pour the milk mixture back into the pan then heat gently, stirring continuously, until almost boiling, and thickened and smooth. Tip back into the bowl and sprinkle with a little extra sugar to prevent a skin forming. Cover, allow to cool, then chill until required.

Serve the tarts and custard cold, or reheat if preferred and dust with a little sifted confectioners' sugar.

For mincemeat & apple tarts with orange custard, top each rectangle of pastry with 1 tablespoon mincemeat, then add half a cored and sliced dessert apple. Bake as above and serve with custard flavored with the grated zest of ½ small orange instead of the saffron.

198

babacos & lime sorbet

Preparation time **15 minutes**,
  plus freezing
Cooking time **10 minutes**
Serves **4**

½ cup **granulated sugar**
⅔ cup **water**
1 lb **babacos** or ripe **papaya**,
  seeded, peeled, and diced
finely grated zest and juice
  of 2 **limes**
lime wedges

Put the granulated sugar in a saucepan with the measured water and heat gently to dissolve the sugar. Increase the heat, bring to a boil, and stop stirring. Boil for 5 minutes. Remove from the heat and allow to cool.

Set aside 2 tablespoons of diced fruit, and put the remainder in a food processor or blender with the cooled sugar syrup. Blend until smooth. Add the lime rind and juice to the puree and pour into a shallow metal container. Freeze for 3 hours.

Remove from the freezer and beat with a fork to break up the ice crystals. Stir in the reserved diced fruit, return to the freezer and freeze until solid.

When ready to serve, remove the sorbet from the freezer and allow to stand for 10 minutes. Scoop into small glasses and serve topped with a lime wedge.

For raspberry sorbet, make the syrup as above then allow to cool. Puree 3¾ cups raspberries, sieve, and mix with the syrup and the grated zest and juice of 1 lemon. Omit the chopped fruit and freeze as above. Serve with extra raspberries.

coconut crème caramel

Preparation time **15 minutes**, plus chilling
Cooking time **30 minutes**
Serves **4**

½ cup **granulated sugar**
½ cup **water**
2 tablespoons boiling **water**
2 **eggs**, plus 2 extra **egg yolks**
2 tablespoons **superfine sugar**
1¾ cups **reduced-fat coconut milk**
½ cup **lowfat milk**
1¼ cups **raspberries**

Heat the granulated sugar and water in a small saucepan, stirring occasionally, until the sugar has just dissolved. Bring to a boil and cook, without stirring, for 5 minutes until golden.

Take the pan off the heat, add the boiling water then stand well back, tilting the pan to mix, until the bubbles have subsided. Divide the caramel between 4 1 cup metal pudding molds, then swirl the caramel over the inside. Put the molds in a roasting pan.

Beat the eggs, egg yolks, and superfine sugar together to mix. Pour the coconut milk and lowfat milk into a saucepan and bring just to a boil, then gradually beat into the eggs. Strain into the molds.

Pour hot (not boiling) water into the roasting pan to come halfway up the sides of the molds. Cover the tops loosely with buttered foil then bake in a preheated oven, 325°F, for 30 minutes until just set. Remove from the oven and leave the molds in the water for 10 minutes. Lift them out, allow to cool then chill for 4 hours or longer until required.

When ready to serve, dip the bases of the molds into boiling water for 10 seconds, loosen, then turn out on to rimmed serving plates. Decorate with raspberries.

For chocolate custard pots, beat 2 eggs, 2 egg yolks, and ¼ cup superfine sugar together. Heat ⅔ cup heavy cream and 1¾ cups milk in a pan with 5 oz semisweet chocolate, stirring until melted. Beat into the eggs then pour into small heatproof dishes. Cook as above for 20–25 minutes. Cool and serve with cream.

gingered treacle tart

Preparation time **30 minutes**
Cooking time **45–55 minutes**
Finishing time **15 minutes**
(optional)
Serves **8**

2 cups **light corn syrup**
2 tablespoons **butter**
finely grated zest and juice
of 1 **lemon**
2¼ cups fresh **bread crumbs**
⅓ cup **crystallized** or **stem
ginger** drained and chopped
2 **dessert apples**, cored and
coarsely grated
1¾ cups **all-purpose flour**
½ cup **butter**, diced
2 tablespoons cold **water**
1 tablespoon **milk**

Tip the corn syrup into a saucepan, add the butter, and heat gently until melted. Stir in the lemon juice, bread crumbs, ginger, and apples then allow to cool.

To make the pastry, put the flour, butter, and lemon zest into a bowl and blend in the butter until the mixture resembles fine bread crumbs. Add the measured water and mix to a smooth dough, adding a little extra water if necessary. Knead lightly, roll out, and use to line a 9½ inch removable-bottomed tart pan. Trim off the excess and reserve.

Pour the syrup mixture into the tart shell. Roll out the pastry trimmings thinly, cut narrow strips and arrange in a lattice, sticking the edges with a little milk. Then glaze all of the strips with milk. Place the tart on a hot baking sheet then bake in a preheated oven, 375°F, for 40–50 minutes until golden and the filling has set. Cover the top loosely with foil after 30 minutes, if necessary, to prevent the tart burning. Set aside until required.

When ready to serve, warm the tart in a preheated oven, 325°F, for 15 minutes or serve cold with clotted cream or vanilla ice cream.

For pecan pie, make up the tart shell as above. Warm ½ cup light corn syrup in a saucepan with 1 cup light brown sugar and ⅓ cup butter until melted. Cool slightly, then beat in 3 eggs and ½ teaspoon vanilla extract. Pour into the tart shell and arrange 1½ cups of pecans on top. Bake at 350°F, for 40–50 minutes until set, covering with foil if needed.

persimmon & star anise jelly

Preparation time **15 minutes**
Cooking time **5 minutes**
Finishing time **5 minutes**
Serves **6**

2½ cups **orange** or **mango juice**
1 **star anise**
⅓ cup **superfine sugar**
2 tablespoons **gelatin**
2 **persimmons**
¾ cup **blueberries**

Measure out 6 tablespoons of the orange or mango juice and set aside. Add the star anise to the remaining juice and the sugar in a saucepan and heat gently for 2–3 minutes, stirring frequently, until the sugar has dissolved. Remove from the heat and allow to stand until cold. Remove and discard the star anise.

Put the reserved orange or mango juice and the gelatin in a small bowl and allow to stand for 5 minutes. Heat over a pan of gently simmering water and leave until the gelatin has dissolved completely.

Remove the gelatin from the heat, allow to cool for 5 minutes and then stir it into the sweetened orange juice. Pour the mixture into a 2½ cup loaf pan or jelly mold or into 6 individual molds. Chill for 20 minutes.

Cut the tops off the persimmons, peel back the skin, and cut the flesh into small dice. Mix the persimmons with the blueberries and stir into the orange or mango jelly which will have begun to set. Return to the refrigerator and chill for 4 hours or until required.

When ready to serve, dip the mold or molds into warm water to loosen the jelly, then turn out onto a plate. Serve topped with physalis, slices of persimmon, and single cream, if desired.

fall berry crumble

Preparation time **10 minutes**
Cooking time **10 minutes**
Finishing time **20 minutes**
Serves **4**

2½ cups **cranberries**
1 cup **blackberries**
1⅓ cups **blueberries**
4 tablespoons **water**
⅓ cup **superfine sugar**

Crumble
1½ cups fresh **bread crumbs**
¾ cup ground **almonds**
⅓ cup **butter**, diced
¼ cup **superfine sugar**
¼ cup slivered **almonds**

Put the fruits into a saucepan with the measured water, cover, and cook over a gentle heat for 10 minutes or until just tender. Stir in the sugar then tip into a shallow ovenproof dish, leaving room for the crumble. Allow to cool, then cover and chill until required.

To make the crumble, put the bread crumbs, ground almonds, butter, and sugar into a bowl and blend the butter in with your fingertips until the mixture resembles fine crumbs. Cover and chill until required.

When ready to serve, break up the crumble and sprinkle over the top of the fruit. Sprinkle with the slivered almonds, then bake in a preheated oven, 375°F, for 20–25 minutes until crisp and golden. Cover with foil after 15 minutes if it is getting too brown. Spoon into bowls and serve with just-melting scoops of vanilla ice cream or hot vanilla custard.

For apple & coconut crumble, peel, core, and slice 1¼ lb cooking apples, and use instead of the berries. Use shredded coconut in place of the ground almonds in the crumble and omit the slivered almonds.

ricotta cake with summer fruits

Preparation time **25 minutes**
Cooking time **40–45 minutes**
Finishing time **5 minutes**
Serves **6**

¾ cup **ricotta cheese**
1 cup **superfine sugar**
1 cup **self-rising flour**
⅔ cup **cornstarch**
2 teaspoons **baking powder**
3 **eggs**, beaten
⅔ cup light **olive oil**, or half
    virgin olive oil and half
    sunflower oil
2 tablespoons **Sambuca**,
    sherry, or **kirsch**

To finish
2 **peaches**, halved, pitted,
    and sliced
1⅛ cups **strawberries**
small bunch of seedless **red**
    grapes, halved
3 tablespoons **Sambuca**,
    sherry, or **kirsch**
sifted **confectioners' sugar**

Mix the ricotta and sugar together in a bowl. In a separate bowl, mix the flour, cornstarch, and baking powder together. Gradually beat alternate spoonfuls of egg and flour into the ricotta until the mixture is smooth.

Gradually beat in the oil in a thin steady trickle, then the liqueur or sherry to make a smooth thick batter. Pour the mixture into a greased and base-lined 9 inch springform cake pan. Level the surface then cook in a preheated oven, 350°C, for 40–45 minutes until well risen and a skewer comes out clean when inserted into the center of the cake. Allow to cool in the pan, cover, and set aside until required.

Mix all the fruits together in a bowl then drizzle over the liqueur or sherry.

When ready to serve, loosen the edge of the cake, transfer to a cutting board and remove the lining paper and pan base. Dust heavily with sifted confectioners' sugar and cut into thin wedges. Serve two per portion with a spoonful of the fruit and a little sour cream.

For orange ricotta cake, use Grand Marnier or Cointreau instead of the liqueur or sherry, adding 1 tablespoon finely grated orange zest to the cake. Serve with orange and blood orange segments drizzled with a little extra orange liqueur.

lemon semifreddo with compote

Preparation time **15 minutes**,
   plus freezing
Cooking time **10 minutes**
Finishing time **5 minutes**
Serves **6**

2½ cups **heavy cream**
¾ cup **superfine sugar**
finely grated zest of **1 lemon**,
   plus juice of 2 lemons

Blackberry compote
2 cups **blackberries**
¼ cup **superfine sugar**
4 tablespoons **water**
1 teaspoon **cornstarch**

Pour the cream into a saucepan, add the sugar, and heat gently, stirring, until the sugar has dissolved. Bring to a boil and cook for 1 minute then take off the heat, stir in the lemon zest, and gradually mix in the strained juice. Pour into a deep nonmetallic dish and allow to cool.

To make the compote, put the blackberries, sugar, and water into a small saucepan. Cover and cook gently for 4–5 minutes until the blackberries are just cooked. Mix the cornstarch with a little water to make a smooth paste. Stir into the blackberries and bring back to a boil, stirring until the sauce has cleared and thickened. Cover and allow to cool.

Freeze the cooled lemon custard for 4–5 hours until just firm and partially frozen. Reheat the compote. Scoop the semifreddo into small bowls or glass tumblers using a hot dessertspoon. Spoon the warm compote over the top and serve immediately with biscotti cookies.

For chilled citrus pots with summer fruits, add ½ cup mixed lemon, lime, and orange juice to the sweetened cream and lemon zest mixture. Chill until set, then serve with mixed summer fruits. This dessert is not frozen.

strawberry & vodka granita

Preparation time **30 minutes**,
  plus freezing
Cooking time **3 minutes**
Finishing time **5 minutes**,
  plus standing
Serves **6**

½ cup **superfine sugar**
1¼ cups **water**
3 cups **strawberries**, hulled,
  plus extra to decorate
4 tablespoons **lemon juice**
6 tablespoons **vodka**

Tip the sugar and water into a small saucepan, heat gently, stirring occasionally, until the sugar has dissolved then bring to a boil and cook for 1 minute.

Puree the strawberries in a blender or food processor until smooth then press through a sieve to remove the seeds. Stir into the sugar syrup with the lemon juice and vodka. Pour into a shallow container so that the syrup is no more than 1 inch deep, cover, and allow to cool.

Transfer the dish to the freezer and freeze for 2 hours until just beginning to set around the edges of the dish. Break up the icy edges with a fork and return to the freezer. Beat with a fork every 30 minutes or so over a 2 hour period until the mixture has formed tiny ice crystals and looks like crushed ice. Freeze until required.

When ready to serve, remove the frozen granita from the freezer and leave at room temperature for 15–30 minutes until soft enough to mix. Spoon into tiny glasses set on small plates and decorate the plates with tiny halved strawberries, if desired. If feeling generous, drizzle with a little extra vodka.

For orange & tequila granita, omit the strawberries and add the juice of 6 oranges and 6 tablespoons tequila instead of the vodka.

iced fig risotto

Preparation time **10 minutes**
Cooking time **40 minutes**
Finishing time **5 minutes**
Serves **4**

2½ cups **milk**
3 tablespoons **superfine sugar**
finely grated zest of **1 orange**
½ cup **risotto rice**
8 fresh **figs**
butter, for greasing
2 tablespoons **honey**
2 tablespoons **orange juice**
1½ cups **vanilla ice cream**

Put the milk, sugar, and orange zest in a large saucepan and bring almost to a boil. Add the rice and cook on the lowest possible heat, stirring frequently, for 25–35 minutes or until the rice is creamy but the grains are still firm. Remove from the heat and set aside to cool. Chill until required.

Meanwhile, halve the figs and place in a lightly buttered shallow ovenproof dish. Drizzle with the honey and orange juice and bake in a preheated oven, 400°F, for 20 minutes, or until beginning to brown. Allow to cool, then chill until required.

When ready to serve, scoop the ice cream into the rice mixture and stir until it has just melted to make a creamy sauce. Spoon into bowls with the figs and cooking juices and garnish with thin slices of orange rind, if desired, and serve immediately.

strawberry syllabub with brittle

Preparation time **20 minutes**
Cooking time **5–7 minutes**
Finishing time **1 minute**
Serves **6**

½ cup **granulated sugar**
3 tablespoons **water**
3 tablespoons slivered
    almonds
3 cups **strawberries**, hulled
1¼ cups **heavy cream**
¼ cup **superfine sugar**
finely grated zest and juice
    of ½ **lemon**
4 tablespoons **white wine**

Put the granulated sugar, water, and almonds into a skillet and heat gently, without stirring, for 2–3 minutes until the sugar has dissolved. Tilt the pan to mix the sugar, if needed. When dissolved, increase the heat and boil the mixture for 3–4 minutes until the syrup and nuts are just turning golden. Tip out onto an oiled baking sheet and allow to cool and harden.

Meanwhile, make the syllabub by pureeing the strawberries in a blender or food processor. Sieve out the seeds, if desired. Whip the cream until it forms soft peaks then beat in the superfine sugar, lemon zest and juice, and wine. Fold in the strawberry puree and divide between 6 glasses, set on a plate. Chill until required.

To serve, lift the almond brittle off the baking sheet and break into shards. Arrange on the syllabub plate and serve immediately.

For peach syllabub with brittle, substitute sesame seeds for the slivered almonds in the brittle. Puree 3 pitted and sliced peaches, then press the puree through a sieve. Make the syllabub as above, using the peach puree instead of the strawberry puree.

mini minted pineapple pavlovas

Preparation time **30 minutes**
Cooking time **about 1 hour**
Finishing time **10 minutes**
Serves **6**

Meringues
3 **egg whites**
¾ cup **superfine sugar**
1 teaspoon **cornstarch**
1 teaspoon **white wine vinegar**
½ teaspoon **vanilla extract**

Filling
4 fresh **pineapple** slices, peeled, cored, and diced
2 tablespoons chopped **mint**, plus extra to decorate
2 tablespoons **superfine sugar**
¾ cup **heavy cream**

To make the meringues, beat the egg whites in a large bowl until stiff then gradually beat in the superfine sugar, a teaspoonful at a time. Beat for a minute or two more until the meringue is very thick and glossy.

Mix the cornstarch, vinegar, and vanilla together in a small dish then beat into the meringue. Spoon the mixture into 6 mounds on a large baking sheet lined with nonstick parchment paper and swirl into circles with the back of the spoon. Bake in a preheated oven, 225°F, for 50–60 minutes or until the meringues can be easily peeled off the paper. Allow to cool on the baking sheet.

Meanwhile, mix the pineapple in a bowl with the chopped mint and superfine sugar. Cover and chill until required.

When ready to serve, whip the cream until softly peaking. Stir the pineapple and fold half the fruit and any juices into the cream. Transfer the pavlovas to serving plates, spoon the cream on top then spoon over the remaining pineapple. Decorate with mint leaves, if desired, and serve within 30 minutes.

For strawberry & cassis pavlovas, make the meringue bases as above. For the filling, mix 2 tablespoons superfine sugar with 2⅔ cups strawberries, sliced, and 2 tablespoons cassis liqueur or elderflower cordial. Add half the strawberries to the cream as above, and top the pavlovas with the remaining strawberries.

pistachio chocolate brownies

Preparation time **25 minutes**
Cooking time **25 minutes**
Finishing time **2–3 minutes**
Serves **6**

7 oz **semisweet chocolate**,
  broken into pieces
1 cup **butter**, diced
1 cup **light brown sugar**
3 **eggs**
½ cup **all-purpose flour**
1 teaspoon **baking powder**
½ cup **pistachio nuts**, roughly
  chopped

Sauce
4 oz **semisweet chocolate**,
  broken into pieces
⅔ cup **lowfat milk**
2 tablespoons **light brown
  sugar**

Melt the chocolate and butter in a large bowl set over a saucepan of gently simmering water. Beat the sugar and eggs with an electric mixer until very thick and the mixer leaves a trail when lifted out of the mixture. Fold in the melted chocolate then the flour and baking powder.

Pour the mixture into an 8 inch square cake pan lined with nonstick parchment paper and sprinkle with the pistachios. Bake in a preheated oven, 350°F, for about 25 minutes until the top is crusty but the center is still slightly soft. Allow to cool and harden in the pan.

To make the sauce, heat the chocolate, milk, and sugar gently in a saucepan, stirring until smooth. Allow to cool, cover, and chill until required.

When ready to serve, lift the brownies out of the pan using the paper. Cut into small squares, lift off the paper and transfer to serving plates. Add scoops of vanilla ice cream and serve with the reheated chocolate sauce.

For white chocolate & cranberry blondies, melt
7 oz white chocolate, broken into pieces, with ½ cup butter. Beat ⅔ cup superfine sugar with 3 eggs as above then fold in the chocolate mixture. Fold in 1¼ cups self-rising flour, and ½ cup dried cranberries. Bake as above.

banoffee cheesecake

Preparation time **30 minutes**,
  plus chilling
Cooking time **about 1 hour**
Finishing time **10 minutes**
Serves **8**

8 oz **graham crackers**
¼ cup **butter**
2½ cups **full-fat cream
  cheese**
⅓ cup **superfine sugar**
⅔ cup **heavy cream**
4 **eggs**
2 ripe **bananas**, peeled
2 tablespoons **lemon juice**
4 oz **toffee candies**,
  unwrapped
1 teaspoon **vanilla extract**

To finish
6 oz **toffee candies**,
  unwrapped
⅔ cup **heavy cream**

Place the crackers in a plastic bag and crush using a rolling pin until they form fine crumbs. Melt the butter in a saucepan then stir in the crumbs and mix well. Tip the mixture into a greased 9 inch springform cake pan and press over the base and up the sides of the pan with the end of a rolling pin.

Bake the crust in a preheated oven, 350°F, for 5 minutes then remove from the oven and allow to cool. Reduce the oven temperature to 300°F.

Beat the cream cheese and sugar together in a bowl then gradually beat in the cream then the eggs, one at a time. Mash the bananas on a plate with the lemon juice, crush the toffee candies, then stir into the cheese mixture with the vanilla extract.

Pour into the cracker crust and bake for 50–60 minutes until the cheesecake is firm around the edges but still a little soft in the center. Turn off the oven and open the door slightly. Allow the cheesecake to cool in the oven for 1 hour then take out and cool completely. Cover and chill for 4–5 hours or overnight until set firm.

When ready to serve, melt two-thirds of the toffee candies in a small saucepan with 2 tablespoons of the cream. Loosen the edge of the cheesecake with a spatula, remove the pan, and transfer to a serving plate. Whip the rest of the cream and spread over the top of the cheesecake. Sprinkle with the rest of the candies, smashed into pieces. Cut into wedges and serve drizzled with the warm toffee sauce.

cidered apple jellies

Preparation time **20 minutes**,
  plus chilling
Cooking time **15 minutes**
Finishing time **5 minutes**
Serves **6**

2 lb **cooking apples**, peeled,
  cored, and sliced
1 ¼ cups **hard cider**
⅔ cup **water**, plus
  4 tablespoons
⅓ cup **superfine sugar**
finely grated zest of 2 **lemons**
4 teaspoons **powdered
  gelatin**
⅔ cup **heavy cream**

Put the apples, cider, ⅔ cup of water, sugar, and the zest of one of the lemons into a saucepan. Cover and simmer for 15 minutes until the apples are soft.

Meanwhile put the 4 tablespoons of water into a small bowl and sprinkle over the gelatin, making sure that all the powder is absorbed by the water. Set aside.

Add the gelatin to the hot apples and stir until completely dissolved. Puree the apple mixture in a blender or food processor until smooth, then pour into 6 tea cups. Allow to cool then chill for 4–5 hours until fully set.

When ready to serve, whip the cream until it forms soft peaks. Spoon over the jellies and sprinkle with the remaining lemon zest.

For cidered apple granita, omit the gelatin and pour the pureed apple mixture into a shallow dish so that the mixture is about 1 inch deep or less. Freeze for about 2 hours until mushy around the edges, then beat with a fork. Freeze for 2 hours more, beating the granita at 30 minute intervals until the texture of crushed ice. Freeze until ready to serve, then scoop into small glasses.

panna cotta with strawberries

Preparation time **20 minutes**, plus chilling
Cooking time **3–4 minutes**
Finishing time **5 minutes**
Serves **6**

3 teaspoons **powdered gelatin**
3 tablespoons cold **water**
1 **vanilla bean**
1¾ cups **heavy cream**
⅔ cup **whole milk**
½ cup **confectioners' sugar**, plus 2 tablespoons
2⅔ cups **strawberries**, roughly chopped
3 tablespoons **Pimms** (optional)
mint leaves

Sprinkle the gelatin over the cold water in a small bowl and set aside for 5 minutes. Meanwhile, slit the vanilla bean along its length and scrape out the seeds with a small knife, add to a saucepan with the bean, cream, milk, and ½ cup of the confectioners' sugar.

Bring the cream mixture to a boil, add the gelatin, take off the heat and stir until the gelatin has completely dissolved. Allow to cool for 20 minutes, stirring from time to time so that a skin doesn't form. Remove the vanilla bean and discard. Divide the vanilla cream between six ⅔ cup individual metal pudding molds. Allow to cool, then chill for 4–5 hours until set.

Mix the strawberries with the remaining sugar and the Pimms, if using. Cover and chill until required.

When ready to serve, dip the bases of the molds into hot water for 10 seconds, then loosen the top edge, invert onto a small plate and jerk to release dessert. Lift off the mold and spoon strawberries around the dessert. Serve decorated with mint leaves.

For strawberry panna cotta with summer berries, omit ⅔ cup of the cream and add 1⅓ cups pureed strawberries instead. Serve with 3 cups mixed summer berries sweetened with a little sugar.

chocolate & cardamom pots

Preparation time **10 minutes**
Cooking time **8 minutes**
Finishing time **5 minutes**
Serves **4**

7 oz good-quality **semisweet chocolate**, broken into squares
seeds from 8–10 **cardamom pods**, crushed
2 tablespoons **coffee liqueur**
2 tablespoons **extra virgin olive oil**
3 large **eggs**, separated
4 tablespoons whipped **cream**
sifted **cocoa powder**

Place the chocolate squares in a small, heatproof bowl with the crushed cardamom, coffee liqueur, and olive oil and set over a pan of barely simmering water. Allow the chocolate to melt very slowly without stirring for about 8 minutes.

Remove the bowl of chocolate from the heat and quickly beat in the egg yolks. Set aside while you put the egg whites in a large bowl and beat until stiff. Stir 1 tablespoon of the beaten whites into the chocolate mixture to slacken it, then carefully fold in the remaining egg whites with a metal spoon.

Divide the mixture between 4 ramekins or pretty coffee cups. Cover and chill for 2 hours, or until required. Serve with whipped cream and a dusting of cocoa powder.

For chocolate brandy pots, omit the cardamom pods and add 2 tablespoons brandy instead of the coffee liqueur. Decorate with chocolate coffee beans.

sweet cheese with berries

Preparation time **25 minutes**
Cooking time **10 minutes**
Finishing time **5 minutes**
Serves **4**

¼ cup **superfine sugar**
3 tablespoons **water**
2–3 fresh **lavender heads**
  (optional)
1 **egg white**
2 cups **Quark** (soft cheese)
¾ cup **sour cream**

Fruit syrup:
2 tablespoons **superfine
  sugar**
2 tablespoons **water**
2 cups mixed **soft fruit**, such
  as **raspberries**, **blueberries**,
  and **blackberries**

Put the superfine sugar and water in a small saucepan and simmer gently until the sugar has dissolved. Add the lavender flowers to the syrup, if using, and simmer for 3 minutes. Remove from the heat and allow to cool.

Beat the egg white in a clean bowl until it stands in stiff peaks. Mix the Quark and sour cream in another bowl, stir in the cold strained lavender syrup, then fold in the beaten egg white.

Line 4 perforated molds or recycled, clean yogurt pots with small holes in the bottom, with damp pieces of cheesecloth and stand the molds on a plate to catch the liquid that will drip out. Spoon the cheese mixture into the molds, level, and chill overnight or until required.

To make the fruit syrup, put the superfine sugar and water in a small saucepan and heat gently to dissolve the sugar. Add half the fruit to the warm syrup and cook for 1 minute, then remove from the heat. When the syrup and fruit are cold, stir in the remaining fruit. Cover and chill until required.

When ready to serve, turn the cheeses out of their molds onto 4 serving plates. Serve with the soft fruits and decorate with mint sprigs.

For quick berry brûlées, divide ¾ cup raspberries and 1 cup blueberries between six ⅔ cup heatproof dishes. Mix ¾ cup sour cream with ¾ cup plain yogurt, 2 tablespoons superfine sugar, and 1 teaspoon vanilla extract. Spoon over the berries. Refrigerate until ready to serve, then sprinkle each dish with 2 teaspoons superfine sugar. Broil until golden.

index

acknowledgments

Executive Editor: Nicky Hill
Senior Editor: Charlotte Macey
Executive Art Editor: Penny Stock
Designer: Joanna Macgregor
Photographer: William Shaw
Home Economist: Sara Lewis
Prop Stylist: Liz Hippisley
Senior Production Controller: Martin Croshaw

Special photography: © Octopus Publishing Group Limited/William Shaw
All other photography: © Octopus Publishing Group Limited.